MW01156080

ORIGINAL
BMW
AIR-COOLED BOXER TWINS

Other titles available in the *Original* series are:

Original AC Ace & Cobra
by Rinsey Mills
Original Aston Martin DB4/5/6
by Robert Edwards
Original Austin Seven
by Rinsey Mills
Original Austin-Healey (100 & 3000)
by Anders Ditlev Clausager
Original Camaro 1972-1986
by Andy Kraushaar and Jason Scott
Original Citroën DS
by John Reynolds with Jan de Lange
Original Corvette 1953-1962
by Tom Falconer
Original Corvette 1963-1967
by Tom Falconer
Original Ducati Sport & Super Sport 1972-1986
by Ian Falloon
Original Ferrari V8
by Keith Bluemel
Original Ferrari V12 1965-1973
by Keith Bluemel
Original Harley-Davidson Panhead
by Greg Field
Original Honda CB750
by John Wyatt
Original Jaguar E-Type
by Philip Porter
Original Jaguar Mark I/II
by Nigel Thorley
Original Jaguar XJ
by Nigel Thorley
Original Jaguar XK
by Philip Porter
Original Land Rover Series I
by James Taylor
Original Mercedes SL
by Laurence Meredith
Original MG T Series
by Anders Ditlev Clausager
Original MGA
by Anders Ditlev Clausager
Original MGB
by Anders Ditlev Clausager
Original Mini Cooper and Cooper S
by John Parnell
Original Morgan
by John Worrall and Liz Turner
Original Morris Minor
by Ray Newell
Original Mustang 1964½-1966
by Colin Date
Original Pontiac GTO 1964-1974
by Tom de Mauro
Original Porsche 356
by Laurence Meredith
Original Porsche 911
by Peter Morgan
Original Porsche 924/944/968
by Peter Morgan
Original Rolls-Royce & Bentley 1946-65
by James Taylor
Original Sprite & Midget
by Terry Horler
Original Triumph TR2/3/3A
by Bill Piggott
Original Triumph TR4/4A/5/6
by Bill Piggott
Original Triumph Stag
by James Taylor
Original Vincent
by J. P. Bickerstaff
Original VW Beetle
by Laurence Meredith
Original VW Bus
by Laurence Meredith

ORIGINAL BMW AIR-COOLED BOXER TWINS 1950–1996

by Ian Falloon

First published in 2003 by MBI Publishing Company, Galtier Plaza, 380 Jackson Street, Suite 200, St. Paul, MN 55101-3885 USA

ISBN 0-7603-1424-1

All photos by Ian Falloon unless otherwise indicated.

Front Jacket: The Daytona Orange R90S epitomizes the finest attributes of the air-cooled boxer twin, and provided Superbike performance in its day.

Frontispiece: An indication of the performance available from the R68 was the 120-mile-per-hour Veigel speedometer.

Title Page: Like the /2, the /5 incorporated the driveshaft inside the right side of the swingarm. This is a late-1971 R60/5, number 2 938 848, ostensibly for the 1972 model year but still with many 1971 components.

Contents: One of the most appealing aspects of an air-cooled boxer twin is that older models, such as this 1977 R100RS, can still provide an exhilarating riding experience. Unlike many motorcycles of the 1970s, they are also extremely reliable, and compared to modern motorcycles the air-cooled boxer is simple, and nonintimidating. *Cycle World*

Rear Jacket
With its groundbreaking full fairing, the R100RS established new standards for motorcycle aerodynamics and rider protection.

Designed by Chris Fayers

Printed in China

Contents

Chapter 1

Postwar Twins through 1969

The R69S was considered by many to represent the end of the classic era for BMW twins. This is a restored 1962 example.

Early in 1923, BMW's chief engineer, Max Friz, took the M2 B15 flat-twin engine, turned it sideways, and added a shaft final drive to produce the R32, the first BMW motorcycle. With its two opposing cylinders sitting out in the cool airflow, and low-maintenance shaft drive, the R32 set the configuration that would define the BMW motorcycle for the next 80 years and beyond. Although at various stages throughout BMW's history the boxer twin has been outsold by singles, or threatened with extinction, it has endured.

While many of the prewar and immediate postwar twins have garnered a strong and loyal following, the twins from 1955, followed by the later /5 series and its descendents, are the most numerous and popular. The Earles fork twins through 1969 are now considered the culmination of the classic era, while the newer series, lasting through 1996, are arguably recognized as the archetypal rendition of the boxer series.

With the /5 series and its later renditions came a new ethos for BMW motorcycles. Although still expensive, they were innovative, and they appealed to a wider market. Yet while the design was new, the /5 continued the design philosophy that began with the R32 and concluded with the /2 series.

In the aftermath of World War II, BMW emerged battered and broken, and it wasn't until 1948 that its first postwar motorcycle appeared. Allied restrictions at the time only allowed for the production of the 250-cc R24, but these limitations

When BMW decided to produce a 500-cc twin for 1950, the R51/2, the company resurrected a prewar design. The sidestand shown was nonstandard, but otherwise this restored version is very original. The deeply valanced front fender was also an R51/2 feature.

were lifted during the summer of 1949. The R24, based on the prewar R23, had already proved extremely successful, and as there was little money available for the development of a larger model, the same formula was used for the first postwar twin. By resurrecting the 1938 R51 overhead-valve twin, BMW created the R51/2. Although its foundations went back even earlier, to the 1936 R5, the R51/2 proved immediately popular when it was released in 1950.

This chapter is an overview of the postwar twins through 1969, briefly covering the less common 1950–54 examples, with more detail on the 1955–69 twins.

Setting the R51/2 apart were the two-piece rocker covers, which were also a feature on the wartime R75. The engine was very similar to the R5 engine of 1936.

R51/2

Apart from the split two-piece valve covers (similar to those of the wartime R75 military motorcycle) and semidowndraft Bing 22-mm carburetors, the engine of the R51/2 was virtually identical to that of the prewar R51. The R51/2 had new cylinder heads with coil, rather than hairpin, valve springs, but the engine layout still included twin camshafts driven by a long timing chain that also drove the generator. This exposed generator included a distinctive finned clamp on top of the engine. The 6-volt ignition was by battery and coil. BMW postwar developments included a coil-spring damper on the gearbox mainshaft, and a revised lubrication system with pressurized oil to the camshaft bearings. The compression ratio was even lower than the prewar R51's, at 6.4:1, but the 500-cc (68x68-mm) engine still produced 24 horsepower, at a slightly higher 5,800 rpm. The exposed chrome-plated driveshaft, on the right, included a universal joint where it met the rear suspension, and a hard rubber puck at the transmission output. The standard final drive ratio was 3.89:1 (9/35); this ratio was also used on the later solo R51/3 and R68. For sidecars, the ratio was 4.57:1 (7/32).

Powering the R51/3 of 1951 was an all-new engine. This powerplant would continue through 1969 with very little development.

Also carried over from the prewar design was the chassis, although the frame was the same as the final 1941 version of the R51, with two additional strengthening tubes. Its telescopic fork gained two-way damping, but the plunger rear suspension remained. A valanced front fender also distinguished the R51/2, as did the pivot control levers, rather than inverted levers. With 19-inch wheels front and rear, and weighing 185 kilograms (407 pounds), the R51/2 provided only moderate performance. Its top speed of around 84 miles per hour (135 kilometers per hour) was similar to the prewar R51's. While the R51/2 filled a void in 1950, a more modern design was required for the boxer twin to survive the next decade and beyond.

1951–56 R51/3, R67, R67/2, and R67/3

The R51/3 replaced the R51/2 in 1951. Although they were visually similar, a new engine distinguished the R51/3. This would become one of the classic BMW engine designs, and would form the basis of all the boxer engines through 1969.

The crankcase was still a tunnel block design, and inside the redesigned, narrower, and smoother engine case was a single camshaft above the crankshaft, now driven by helical gears instead of the long chain. The crankshaft was still a built-up type, with two ball bearings at the front and a ball bearing at the rear. Connecting rods ran on roller bearings. Instead of battery ignition, the R51/3 used a Noris magneto mounted on the end of the crankshaft, with the ignition contact breaker and automatic advance at the front of the camshaft. A third gear drove the oil pump, now under the crankshaft rather than in the bottom of the crankcase.

The new engine was also easily identifiable by the six-ribbed one-piece valve covers that would feature on touring 500- and 600-cc models through 1969. Underneath these covers were new cylinder heads, with 34- and 32-mm valves set at an 80-degree angle. Pistons each had four rings. Completing the smooth appearance was a special casing, which contained the paper-element air filter, above the new transmission housing.

The R51/3 may have had a new engine, but with a 6.3:1 compression ratio, the power output of 24 horsepower was unchanged. Also similar was the four-speed gearbox with auxiliary hand lever. BMW carried over the chassis from the R51/2, although it did strengthen the half-hub front

All touring-model twins from 1951 through 1969 had one-piece six-finned aluminum rocker covers.

brake casting. It also increased fuel capacity to 4.5 gallons (17 liters), from 3.5 gallons (14 liters). All these changes resulted in a weight increase to 418 pounds (190 kilograms).

The success of the R51/2 and R51/3 prompted the release of a 600-cc version, the R67, also for 1951. The R67 was not designed as a higher performance sporting model, in the vein of the prewar R66; the R67 was rather staid, and primarily intended for sidecar use. The 594-cc engine had a bore and stroke of 72x73 mm, but an even lower compression ratio of 5.6:1 and two Bing 24-mm carburetors provided only 26 horsepower at 5,500 rpm. The R67 also featured a higher final drive ratio, 1:3.56 (9/32), or 1:4.38 (8/35) with a sidecar.

For 1952 BMW gave the R51/3 a 200-mm two-leading-shoe front brake and rubber gaiters on the front fork instead of prewar-style steel covers. BMW gave the R67 the same updates and renamed it the R67/2. The R67/2's compression ratio was increased to 5.6:1, resulting in a moderate power increase to 28 horsepower at 5,600 rpm. Despite the added power, the 422-pound (192-kilogram) R67/2 was still no road burner.

An exposed chrome-plated driveshaft and auxiliary hand gear shift lever distinguished the pre-1955 twins.

For 1954, the final year of production for the R51/3 and R67/2, BMW gave both of its twins a full-width two-leading-shoe front brake, light alloy 19-inch wheel rims, a new air filter cover, and mufflers without a fishtail. Both models were replaced for 1955 with new models featuring an Earles fork and swingarm rear suspension: the R50 and R69. A black fuel tank with rubber kneepads, and a sprung solo Pagusa saddle with rear rack distinguished all the twins of this period. BMW continued to make refinements, with a myriad of small modifications regularly appearing without official notification.

Even after the advent of the Earles fork R50 and R69 in 1955, BMW continued producing a version of the old R67—the R67/3—as a budget model designed for police forces. BMW built the R67/3, the final model to retain the plunger rear end, for 1955 and 1956. Despite a 4.00x18-inch rear tire to make it even more suitable for sidecar attachment, the R67/3 was one of the least popular postwar twins.

Also from the prewar twins came the plunger rear suspension, which was better than a rigid rear end but not really sufficient for the 1950s.

R68

The demand for more performance in the early 1950s resulted in one of the finest BMW motorcycles of any era, the R68. By 1951, BMW needed a sporting flagship to compete with the new Triumph and BSA parallel twins. In creating the new R68 engine, BMW hot-rodded the pedestrian R67 engine to provide a claimed top speed of 100 miles per hour (161 kilometers per hour). Here was a true successor to the R66 of 1938. The

R68 was a superb sporting machine, which began a tradition of off-road competition boxer twins that eventually led to the R80 G/S in 1980.

That off-road tradition actually began in 1951, while the R68 was in development, when the Fédération des Industries Mécaniques (FIM) lifted the ban on German manufacturers competing in international competition. BMW entered three factory R51/3 racers in the International Six Days Trials (ISDT) at Varese, Italy. Three factory R51/3 racers were prepared for veteran George "Schorsch" Meier, Walter Zeller, and Felix Kraus, and this initiated regular factory involvement in the ISDT and other off-road events for the next 30 years. The 1951 ISDT bikes featured a special high-rise Hoske two-into-one exhaust system, which was included on the first R68 displayed at the end of 1951. By the time production began, BMW had decided to fit a fishtail exhaust as standard, but the company offered the high-rise system as an optional accessory.

Setting the R68 engine apart from the touring R67 engine were higher compression (8:1) pistons, 38- and 34-mm valves with 8-mm (rather than 7-mm) stems, a hotter camshaft, rockers pivoting on needle rollers (after number 650 304) under the new twin-rib valve covers, a barrel-shaped roller bearing for the rear of the crank-

A BMW twin to covet was the magnificent R68, especially when fitted with the optional ISDT high-rise exhaust system.

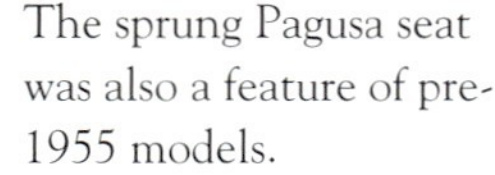

The sprung Pagusa seat was also a feature of pre-1955 models.

An indication of the performance available from the R68 was the 120-mile-per-hour Veigel speedometer.

The final R68 of 1954 featured a full-width front brake, larger headlight, light-alloy wheel rims, and nonfinned mufflers.

With its twin-finned rocker covers, the R68 engine eventually made it into the R69 and R69S. The finned exhaust clamps were also an R68 feature, as was the small front fender.

shaft, and 26-mm carburetors. The twin-rib rocker covers would last through 1977, and then would be resurrected for the R100R of 1992. Also specific to the R68 were finned exhaust nuts, and a manual spark-control lever on the handlebar clutch-lever casting. This allowed for 10 degrees of retardation and easier starting. All these updates increased power to 35 horsepower (from 26) at 7,000 rpm.

The R68 chassis was essentially identical to that of the touring R67/2, but included a narrow sporting front fender, a rear chrome grab handle, and an optional sprung pillion pad, primarily to allow the rider to adopt a more prone riding position. The 19-inch wheels and 200-mm two-leading-shoe brakes were the same as those of the 1952 R51/3. The R68 weighed in at 418 pounds (190 kilograms).

There were a few changes for 1953. By late 1952 rubber gaiters appeared on the front forks, and the mufflers were now nonfinned. BMW added a sidecar mount to the frame after July 1953, and for 1954, added light alloy wheel rims, a full-width front brake, and a larger headlamp.

BMW marketed the R68 as an exclusive sports and recreation machine, not mere transportation, and charged a premium for it, continuing a BMW tradition of exclusivity. BMW advertising made

The RS54 racer of 1953 was the first BMW motorcycle built with Earles forks, but there was little shared with any production model. The complex nature of the engine, with bevel gear–driven overhead camshafts made it horrendously expensive to manufacture.

RS54

Although not widely available, the most exclusive production BMW was the RS54 racer. (RS was short for Rennsport, German for "racing sport.") Designed as an affordable competitive racing motorcycle, primarily for German riders, the RS54 became available in 1953. Although only 24 were produced, the engine formed the basis for the highly successful sidecar racers that won 19 World Championships between 1954 and 1974.

Many of the basic features of the RS54 were inherited from the prewar 500-cc Kompressor (a supercharged racing machine). This included the 66x72-mm bore and stroke, and the close-coupled twin overhead camshafts on each cylinder driven by bevel gears. There were only two main crankshaft bearings, and as the cylinders were offset, the bevel drive lined up with the exhaust camshaft on the right and the inlet on the left. The second camshaft coupled directly to the driven shafts. The cams were too close together to actuate the valves directly, so rockers were used, resulting in a wide included valve angle of 82 degrees. It was an expensive and complicated engine, but a beautifully constructed one. Although the factory racing machines were more highly tuned, the production RS54 had a low 8:1 compression ratio, and with twin Fischer-Amal 30-mm carburetors produced only 45 horsepower at 8,000 rpm.

Compared to the production models of 1953, the RS54 also had a new frame, with an oval-section top tube, duplex loops, and swingarm suspension front and rear. At the front, BMW fitted an Earles pattern leading-link-type fork. A swingarm with the drive shaft enclosed in the right fork arm took care of suspension in the rear. The RS54 weighed only 286 pounds (130 kilograms), but it was not an effective solo racer, limited by the high and wide engine and the excessive unsprung weight and steering inertia of the Earles fork This did not deter Walter Zeller, who finished second in the 1956 500-cc World Championship on a short-stroke factory version.

no apology for the price. As a lifestyle product, the R68 may have been 50 years ahead of its time, but between 1952 and 1954 it only found 1,453 buyers. Today the R68 is one of the most desirable production BMW motorcycles of any era, and certainly from the 1950–54 period. This is not only because it is rare. The R68 was one of the highest performing machines of its time, and one of the best looking.

1955–60 R50, R69, and R60 Earles Fork Twins

BMW finally moved beyond the prewar era with the release of two new twins for 1955, the R50 and R69. As the plunger frame and relatively unsophisticated telescopic fork were obsolete, the R50 and R69 were given a new chassis, incorporating the swingarm front and rear suspension of the racing RS54, that would characterize BMW twins through 1969. As the R67/3 continued for 1955, there was no touring 600 until 1956.

Engine and Transmission

The engine of the R50 was essentially that of the R51/3, but with four-ring (rather than five-ring) pistons providing a slightly higher compression

An identification plate on the headstem detailed each individual motorcycle.

Although the R69 continued with the previous R68 engine, the chassis was completely new. This is an R69S; the bulge in the front generator cover was for the vibration damper.

ratio (6.8:1), and two Bing 1/24/45-46 carburetors. As on earlier BMW engines, the R50's cast-iron cylinders had round fins, a feature that would characterize the 500 models through 1969. Previous BMW 500s used I-section con-rods, but the R50's rods had sword-shaped shanks. Power output increased slightly, to 26 horsepower. The R69 retained the higher performance R68 engine, along with the barrel-shaped rear crankshaft roller bearing, 38- and 34-mm valves with 8-mm stems, pointed cylinder fins, identical Bing 1/26/9-10 carburetors, and the manual ignition control.

New for both the R50 and R69 was the three-shaft (instead of earlier two-shaft) gearbox and diaphragm-spring clutch. The external hand lever disappeared, and the four-speed gearbox featured an improved input shaft shock absorber and all-new ratios.

For 1956, the R60 replaced the R67/3 as the basic 600-cc tourer and sidecar hauler, combining the R67's 28-horsepower engine (but with different Bing 1/24/95-96 carburetors) with the double-swingarm chassis from the R69. All twins from 1955 included a paper Micronic air filter, with the earliest R50 and R69 featuring the two-piece silver canister of the 1954 models. In 1958, the air filter cover received a rounded top. The exhaust system was also modified to include longer and fatter mufflers, with quieter mufflers fitted from December 1955, in response to new German regulations.

Electrical System

Also carried over from the 1954 twins were the 6-volt electrical system and Noris MZ ad/R magneto ignition with automatic advance. The Noris 60/6/1500L generator was basically unchanged, producing a meager 60 watts, while a rather weak 8-Ah battery powered the electrical system. The speedometer and all major electrical components were located in the Hella headlight shell. The lights and electrical system may have been weak, but the magneto ignition system was reliable and required only periodic greasing of the cam and maintenance of the magneto safety spark gap. The magneto fired the same Bosch W240T1 spark plugs as used on the 1950–54 twins.

Chassis

The twin-swingarm chassis of the R50, R60, and R69 represented the biggest improvement over the R51/3 and R68. Its front suspension was a development of the leading-link swingarm type of fork developed by Ernie Earles in England. BMW first used an Earles fork on the RS54 and manufactured them under license from Earles. Although not widely accepted except for sidecars, Earles forks didn't dive excessively under braking and provided an improved ride.

The fork legs angled back and downward, from the steering head to a swingarm pivot behind the front wheel. Unlike those of the RS54, however, the fork legs of the R50, R60, and R69 were straight rather than curved. The swingarm pivoted on a fixed axle attached to the fork legs, and two Boge hydraulic shock absorbers connected the swingarm to the lower fork crown. BMW included two positions for the top shock attachment, one for solo, and a lower one for sidecar use, which increased the trail. The automotive-type Boge hydraulic shock absorbers were more advanced than those on the 1950–54 twins, with progressively wound springs, adjustable through integral short levers on the rear. These forks gave the new BMWs improved ride and less dive under braking than the earlier BMW telescopic fork.

Tapered roller bearings located both the front and rear swingarm pivots, but there was no provision for their lubrication, and they required tedious removal every 7,000 miles (11,270 kilometers).

The driveshaft was now enclosed in the right side of the swingarm, with the universal joint moved to the gearbox end of the driveshaft to cope with the increased travel and a sliding spline at the rear drive end. New final drive ratios were 1:3.18 (11/35) for solo motorcycles and either 1:4.25 (8/34) or 1:4.33 (6/26) for sidecar-equipped motorcycles. When the R60 became available in 1956, it was given a higher ratio than the R50 and R69, at 1:2.91 (11/32) for solo use and 1.386 (7/27) for sidecar use.

Despite the addition of swingarm rear suspension, the frame still resembled the earlier plunger type, but with supports for the swingarm, steel cups locating the shock absorbers, and a slightly thicker central spine and steering head. From October 1955, BMW added a sidestand lug to the R50 frame (after number 552 230). The frame then remained virtually unchanged through 1969. A single key operated the fork lock on the left side of the steering head and the toolbox in the left side of the fuel tank. Steering head bearings were still the loose-ball type in pressed-in cups. Considering the quality of the rest of the components, these obsolete steering head bearings seemed an anomaly, and they compromised handling.

The new BMWs rolled on wheels consisting of 2.15Bx18-inch alloy rims front and rear (with a wider 2.75Cx18-inch rear wheel available for sidecar use), straight-pull spokes of 3.5-mm diameter and finished in dull chrome, and aluminum drums with full-width iron brake liners. To ensure front and wheel interchangeability the tires were 3.50x18-inch, and only Metzeler tires were initially specified.

The new fuel tank was more rounded than those on earlier BMWs and held 4.5 gallons (17 liters). It included a single one-piece Everbest petcock with a junction to each carburetor. A larger sporting 6.5-gallon (25-liter) tank was an option, and this tank had the toolbox lid in the top, rather than the side.

Six optional seats were available for the new twins ranging from a Denfeld solo seat, initially with a short vertical spring but later with rubber "silent-blocs," to a twin Schorsch Meier or Denfeld seat. These were either narrow or wide with passenger grab handles. Most U.S. examples through 1969 featured the narrower dual seat.

The front fender, now pressed steel with a riveted flat steel center brace, no longer incorporated the stand/brace of the R51/3 and R67 that allowed for easier front wheel removal. Also new were the improved geared rack-and-pinion throt-

Imparting a unique look to the 1955–69 twins were the Earles forks. Although they worked satisfactorily, they were more suitable for sidecar use than for solo use.

R50, R60, and R69 Production

Model	Dates	Total
R50	1955–60	13,510
R60	1956–60	17,306
R69	1955–60	2,956
		33,772

tle assembly and two types of Magura chromed handlebar. A narrow European bar and wider 28-inch (71-cm) U.S. version that included a cross-brace. They attached to the fork tops with split one-piece angle risers.

A larger Hella taillight appeared in 1957, but between 1955 and 1960 there was virtually no development to the Earles fork twins. The company was in crisis and sold considerably fewer of its expensive twins than the more affordable R25/3 and subsequent R26 single. Total motorcycle production slumped to only 5,429 in 1957 from 29,699 in 1954, as unsold stock languished in showrooms.

1961–69 R50/2, R60/2, R50S, and R69S

The success of the BMW 700 car with its motorcycle-derived flat twin engine provided the optimism for further development of BMW's motorcycles for 1961, resulting in the R50/2, R50S, R60/2, and R69S, which replaced the earlier twins. Although the new machines looked outwardly similar, they all were powered by engines that had been updated internally for greater reliability. The range-leading R69 became the R69S, and was joined by a sporting R50S, although this model was short-lived.

Engine and Transmission

Inside the engine for the /2 and S were new cam followers, a stronger crankshaft and camshaft, stronger bearing housings, and a new clutch. Crankshafts now had a 20-mm-diameter end taper for the new generator. New three-ring pistons, with all three hard-chromed piston rings above the wrist pin, were used in all the twins.

On the post-1955 twins there was a new gearbox, and the driveshaft was enclosed. Under the rubber bellows was a universal joint. The large air filter canister indicates this is an R69S.

Those used in the R60/2 provided a higher 7.5:1 compression ratio. This resulted in an increase to 30 horsepower at 5,800 rpm for the R60/2. The R50/2 engine specifications were unchanged from the R50, and this was now the most popular model in the two-cylinder lineup.

The R50/2 may have been the biggest seller, but the most exciting new models were the R50S and R69S. The general engine specifications for the R69S were similar to the R69, but for higher compression pistons (9.5:1), larger inlet ports, and a larger volume air filter with a new canister. Also improved was the crankcase ventilation, with the S models receiving a rotary-disc crankcase ventilator. The R50S had slightly smaller valves than the 34- and 32-mm valves of the R69S, with 7-mm stems for the intake and 8-mm for the exhaust, and Bing 1/26/71-72 carburetors. The S model also had a larger-diameter exhaust tip on the less-restrictive muffler, and the power of the R69S was the most yet seen from a production BMW twin, at 42 horsepower at 7,000 rpm. The R50S produced the same power as the earlier R69, 35 horsepower, but at a frenetic 7,650 rpm.

Despite featuring a stronger rear spherical-roller main bearing, both the S models initially suffered from unreliability, with cylinders breaking and wrist pins floating loose. The R50S model was discontinued during 1962; production amounted to a mere 1,634 examples. The company addressed the R69S's reliability problems in 1962 by fitting new pistons with shorter wrist pins (after number 656812), reinforced cylinders (from number 656529), and an engine breather plate with 6-mm (instead of 5-mm) pins (from 656270). BMW added a rubber-mounted vibration damper to the front of the R69S crankshaft from September 1963. This was a large steel disc mounted on a vulcanized ring and fitted on the crankshaft taper between the front engine cover and generator. Unfortunately, the frequent maintenance required to prevent the rubber core from disintegrating was a source of irritation.

The /2 engine required remarkably few changes during the 1960s, because the initial design work on the engine was so sound, In July 1965 the R50/2 received longer pushrods (9.6 inches [243.5 mm] instead of 9.5 inches [242 mm]). All models were fitted with rotating valves after October 1966 (from R50/2 number 641473, R60/2 number 629956 to number 630000 and from number 1810001, and R69S number 661545). From April 1967 (after R50/2 644184 and R60/2 number 1812245), the bolt sleeves in the cylinder heads were made with larger bearing surfaces to prevent migration, with a consequent reduction in valve clearance. The crankshaft was also modified with a wider central cheek during 1967. Problems with spark plug hole threads stripping were solved after September 1968 with new long-reach steel spark plug inserts and longer-reach Bosch W240T2 spark plugs.

BMW reused its existing four-speed gearbox design for its /2 and S twins, but fitted it with closer ratios. New ratios one through three were 1:4.17, 1:2.73, and 1:1.94. Only the 1:1.54 top gear remained the same. It was a sturdy and durable transmission, but it was also noisy and clunky to shift. These problems persisted, even after BMW reduced the endplay in the transmission shafts, starting in September 1966 for the R69S (after number 662545) and June 1967 for the R50/2 and R60/2 (after R50/2 number 643990 and R60/2 1814026). The company claimed that this change reduced the volume at idle on the R69S from 84 to 78 decibels The radii of the cam plate were enlarged after July 1968, accompanied by modifications to the output-shaft shifting pegs (from R50/2 number 646686, R60/2 number 1816037, and R69S number 664451). Even as late as November 1969, there were attempts to improve the gear shift by changing the diameter of the detent spring.

BMW improved the clutch of the 600-cc models with reinforced springs, starting in June 1964 (after R69S number 658624 and R60/2 numbers 626401). A redesigned speedometer helical gear was fitted starting in October 1965 (after R50/2 number 640039, R60/2 number 727956, and R69S number 660144) to eliminate oil leaks.

Final drive ratios were initially 1:3.375 (8/25) for the R69S and R60/2 and 1:3.18 (11/35) for the R50/2. The R50S had a 1:3.58 (7/25). All sidecar ratios were 1:4.33 (6/26) except for the R60/2 1:3.86 (7/27). To prevent oil seepage in hot weather, BMW improved venting of the R69S rear drive case with a cast-in vent plug starting in January 1963 (from number 657099). In July 1968 (from R50/2 646686, R60/2 1816268, and R69S 664651) a new final drive ratio, 1:3.13 (8/27), became standard, coinciding with the larger 4.00x18-inch rear tire.

Carburetors and Air Cleaners

BMW reused the R50's Bing 1/24/45-46 carburetors on the R50/2. The company used new Bing 1/24/125-126 carburetors on the R60/2, Bing 1/26/75-76 carburetors on the R69s, and Bing 1/26/71-72 carburetors on the R50S. To improve starting and cure uneven idle, BMW fitted new float guides, short float ticklers, and revised main jets, starting in June 1967.

Starting in August 1967, BMW changed to the following new carburetors: Bing 1/26/91-92 on the R69S (from number 663 245), Bing 1/24/125-126 on the R60/2 (from number 1814032), and Bing 1/24/149-150 on the R50/2 (from number 645590). These new carburetors

The rear Boge shock absorbers incorporated handles for spring preload adjustment.

All BMW emblems prior to 1966 featured serif lettering.

included recalibrated main jets, offset fuel intake hoses, and black plastic tickler caps instead of metal caps. A Micro-Star paper air filter was now standard, and the air filter canisters on the R50/2 and R60/2 were modified to omit the sliding choke levers.

Electrical System

While the basic 6-volt electrical system was unchanged, a Bosch magneto and Bosch LJ/CGE 60/6/1700RS generator were new for the /2. The ignition was also as before, but Beru 240/14 spark plugs were also specified alongside Bosch, with the S models having Bosch W260T1 or Beru 260/14. The R69S no longer had the manual ignition control that the R69 inherited from the R68.

Chassis

The new /2 and S models inherited their chassis from the previous R69, R60, and R50 models, but with a hydraulic steering damper on the R69S and R50S. In 1962, BMW added reinforcing gussets on the frame downtubes near the battery carrier. Starting with R69S number 656276, small triangular frame gussets were welded to the vertical tubes of the rear swingarm pivots. From April 1962 all frames included drilled-out pivot posts that allowed greasing the rear swingarm bearings, one of the more practical improvements. Along with the introduction of the vibration damper on the R69S, BMW flattened the conical tube cross-brace on the front fork to clear the new front engine cover. From June 1964 (after R50/2 number 636591, R60/2 number 626361, and R69S number 658624), a funnel-type grease fitting was installed to lubricate the front swingarm bearing.

Wheels for the /2 and S models were given thicker 4.0-mm spokes, some in dull-finish chrome, and others in mirror-finish chrome. The 18-inch wheel rims were either chrome-plated steel or aluminum. The tires were 3.50x18-inch front and rear until July 1968 (R50/2 number 646685, R60/2 number 1816267, and R69S number 664650), when a larger 4.00x18-inch tire became standard. Continental tires were now also specified in addition to Metzeler.

The /2 and S series looked very similar to the previous BMW twins. In 1962, BMW started differentiating its flagship twin with "R69S" emblems on the rear fender. The fuel tanks, large and small, were also unchanged, but after 1966 there were new enamel fuel tank emblems with the "BMW" lettering changed to sans-serif type. Paint options for the /2 and S models included black, purewhite, Bavarian Cream, and two variations of red, teal, blue, and green.

U.S. models still had the higher and wider handlebars. Starting in 1967 (after R50/2 number

Most twins from 1955 to 1969 came with a small gas tank and a narrow, full-length seat. This R69S of 1962 has low sporting handlebars, although many U.S. examples had higher handlebars.

The Bing 26-mm carburetors of the R69S were similar to early versions. The zinc-alloy float chamber was cast integrally with the carburetor body.

641437, R60/2 number 629956 to 630000 and after number 1810001, R69S number 661045), all the handlebar levers were a new Magura type with notches and balls. They had nylon bushes in the pivots, and the handlebar switches were redesigned at this time to accept Hella bar-end turn signals.

The Earles fork twins were never mainstream motorcycles, and by the end of the 1960s were generally considered antiquated and obsolete. Virtually unchanged for more than a decade, they were relatively heavy at 444 pounds (202 kilograms) and their performance was sedate. Although the R69S was capable of around 108 miles per hour (175 kilometers per hour), its steering and handling characteristics were idiosyncratic. Their heavy frames and strong Earles fork were designed for sidecar attachment, but sidecars were now out of fashion.

In an effort to provide an updated feel for the United States, always a prime market, in 1967 BMW started building unique versions with a telescopic fork specific for the U.S. market. These were never greeted with much enthusiasm, however.

Ironically, the Earles fork models are now the most sought after, particularly the R69S. Although not especially rare, the R69S embodies

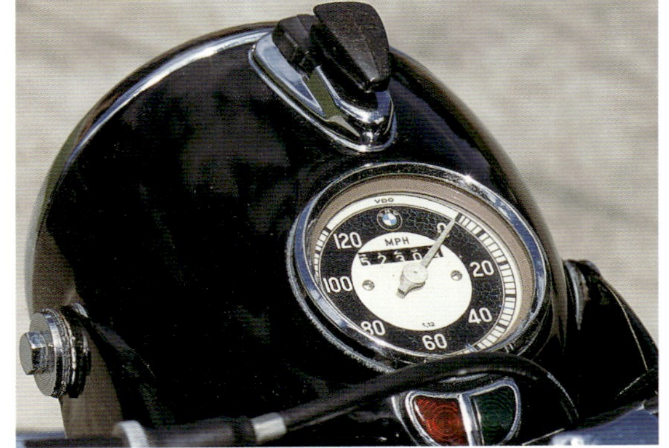

A carryover from the pre-1954 twins through 1969 was the headlight-mounted speedometer (now a VDO) and plunger ignition switch. This is a 1962 R69S. Below left: The /2-series BMWs included very basic Hella handlebar switches.

While this R60/2 looked virtually identical to the earlier R60, inside the engine were a number of improvements aimed at increasing reliability. The power was also increased slightly. This 1961 example has the larger gas tank with the toolbox in the top.

Also distinguishing the R69S were mufflers with a larger exhaust opening. Many R69Ss also came with chromed-steel wheel rims, but the spokes were slightly thicker than those of the R69.

Most R69Ss had this emblem on the rear fender.

the finest qualities that distinguish the pre-/5 twins. With its built-up crankshaft, predominance of ball and roller bearings, and gear-driven camshaft, the engine was a jewel, yet the R69S (and all /2s) remains an eminently practical and useable classic motorcycle. Alongside the R68, the R69S has justifiably earned a place as one of the most desirable postwar BMW motorcycles.

R50/2, R60/2 and R69S Production 1960–69 Model Years

Model	Dates	1960-61	1962	1963	1964	1965	1966	1967	1968	1969	Total
R50/2	01/61-08/69	2,820	1,150	1,468	3,817	2,131	2,557	2,464	1,188	1,040	18,635
R50S	08/60- 8/62	1,050	584								1,634
R60/2	01/60-12/69	1,480	700	1,050	1,955	2,307	2,698	2,615	1,830	792	15,427
R69S	01/60-12/69	1,270	1,068	825	1,300	1,581	1,416	1,420	1,113	321	10,314
											46,010

1967–69 R50US, R60US, and R69US

A belated and almost half-hearted effort to update the /2 appeared from 1967 with three specific U.S. market models, the R50US, R60US, and R69US. The U.S. models were similar in specification to their Earles fork brothers, except that a front telescopic fork replaced the Earles leading-link type and the sidecar lugs were removed from the frame members. As BMW had used telescopic forks on its ISDT machines from 1963, the incorporation of this front suspension on the production twins wasn't unexpected. By 1969 all BMW motorcycles exported to the United States had telescopic forks.

The 36-mm BMW-designed leading axle telescopic fork was very sophisticated for its day. It provided progressive rebound and compression damping through a tapered hydraulic metering rod, and a considerable 8.4 inches (214 mm) of travel. Its biggest advantage over the Earles fork was lighter weight, leading to a reduction in unsprung weight and lowering overall weight to 438 pounds (199 kilograms) for the R69US and 429 pounds (195 kilograms) for the R50US and R60US. The fork featured 13-rib rubber gaiters and a new front fender with tubular steel fork brace. The 200-mm front drum brake was identical to that of the Earles fork twins, with the

Imparting an imposing, if somewhat staid, presence, the R69S was considered obsolete by 1969. It is now one of the classic postwar BMWs. This example has Hella bar-end indicators.

backing plate secured by a long aluminum brace.

The new fork increased the wheelbase slightly, to 56.2 inches (1,427 mm) from 55.7 inches (1,415 mm), with the overall length increasing to 84.1 inches (2,137 mm). Because the steering head was higher, the overall height went up to 39.2 inches (995 mm) for the R69US and 38.6 inches (980 mm) for the other two models, and a taller centerstand and longer sidestand were necessary. Overall, the telescopic fork gave better high-speed performance on bumpy roads, but at the expense of heavier low-speed steering. The R69US retained the hydraulic steering damper, and all U.S. models came with a 4.00x18-inch rear tire.

This attempt to bring the /2 into the 1960s was largely unsuccessful. The telescopic fork couldn't disguise the BMW twins' ancient ancestry, and the price of $1,648 made the R69US the most expensive 600-cc motorcycle available in 1969. Motorcycle production, which had peaked at 9,071 in 1966, dwindled to only 5,074 in 1968. As BMW accelerated its development and manufacture of automobiles, the company considered quitting the motorcycle business. The motorcycle business had covered automotive losses in the early 1960s, but by late in the decade the roles were reversed, and motorcycle production was now unprofitable.

R50US, R60US, and R69US Production 1967–69

Model	Dates	1967	1968	1969	Total
R50US	08/67-08/69	199	132	70	401
R60US	01/67-12/69	708	728	443	1,879
R69US	01/67-12/69	490	83	430	1,003
					3,283

Chapter 2

R75/5, R60/5, and R50/5 (1970–73)

After nearly a decade of developmental stagnation and stumbling sales, toward the end of 1969 BMW decided to release an all-new series of flat-twin motorcycles. Although continuing the traditional two-cylinder boxer layout, both the engine and chassis represented a significant departure from the previous M268 design, and would remain in production until 1996. Coinciding with the release of the new boxer, known as the "stroke-five" or "slash-five," BMW moved motorcycle production from its Munich-Milbertshofen plant to a new facility at Berlin-Spandau.

Technical director Helmut Werner Bönsch wasn't about to let BMW's tradition of building motorcycles die. He managed to persuade the management to allow the development of a new luxury motorcycle that would maintain BMW's reputation for building the finest quality motorcycles available.

Headed by Günter von der Marwitz, the team developing the new /5 set out to produce a modern high-performance motorcycle with outstanding handling. When it was released at Hockenheim on August 28, 1969, even the skeptics were impressed. The /5 was available in three capacities—500, 600, and 750 cc—with the R75/5 the first official 750-cc BMW twin since the military R75 of 1942–44. BMW commenced production of the R60/5 at Spandau in September 1969, with the R75/5 following in October and the R50/5 in November.

The /5 series was an instant sales success. During 1970, BMW sold 12,346 of the /5 series—

With the /5, BMW created a motorcycle that was a significant departure from the earlier Earles fork models. This is a long-wheelbase 1973 R75/5 (chassis number 4002518), with optional chrome-plated battery covers from the 1972 version. The large engine protection bars were also optional.

the strongest motorcycle sales for the company since 1955—and the future of the /5 was secure. The first /5s reached the U.S. East Coast in January 1970 and the West Coast in February, and most of these were R75/5s. Only a few R50/5s were sold in the United States.

1970 R75/5, R60/5, and R50/5

As the /5 was an all-new model, little was carried over from the earlier /2s and R69S. The design was also so sound that only minimal changes were necessary to keep the engine current until its demise at the end of 1996. The main features of the engine are covered in detail in this chapter, with later developments included in the appropriate chapters. It is worth noting that there can be inconsistency in the specification of individual machines, because updated parts were often only installed after the earlier stocks were depleted. This is a feature that still characterizes BMW motorcycles today, but was particularly evident on the /5 series. The variety of components fitted to the /5 can make it very difficult to accurately state whether a part was original or not.

For purposes of identification and development, it is useful to categorize machines by model year, running from September of one year to August of the next. Model identification is also through the chassis number, which is identical to the engine number.

Engine and Drivetrain

BMW's designation for the air-cooled boxer engine in the /5 series and subsequent series was M04*, and within the company it was referred to as the 246. While adhering to the basic principles of its predecessor, the design differed significantly in detail and execution. Not only was the crankshaft now a one-piece forged type running in plain main bearings, the single camshaft was also located below the crankshaft. Not exactly a new idea, this arrangement had been proposed by Leonhard Ischinger in the prototype M205 through M208 500- to 800-cc twins of 1932. These extremely advanced designs, which also featured a one-piece tunnel crankcase and forged crankshaft with plain bearings, never reached the production line.

As the camshaft of the Type 246 engine was now underneath the crankshaft, the pushrods were also below the cylinders, and unlike the earlier engine (which featured a gear camshaft drive), the camshaft was driven by a duplex chain. Engines of the three /5 variants were identical, sharing the same stroke but with different bores. With carburetors and oil, but without ignition coils and an induction system, the R50/5 engine weighed 129 pounds (58.5 kilograms), the R60/6 engine 140 pounds (63.5 kilograms), and the R75/5 engine 143 pounds (64.9 kilograms).

Drive from the crankshaft was still similar to that of the R69S, transferred to the transmission by a single-plate dry clutch mounted to the flywheel. The transmission was a three-shaft four-speed, with output through a universal joint to the drive shaft in the right-side swingarm tube, to a set of spiral bevel gears in the enclosed rear drive.

Crankcase

In the manner of all boxer twins since the R5, the engine housing of the /5 was a one-piece tunnel type, but it was much bulkier than its predecessor as it incorporated an electric starter motor and air filter above the crankcase. Internal gussets reinforced the cast-aluminum housing, and the engine number was located on the engine block, on the left above the oil filler. A BMW logo was stamped after the seven-digit number. The very earliest crankcase housing (July 1969) featured "BMW" lettering cast above the cylinder, as on the /2 series (and carried a different part number), but from 1970 there was a standardized crankcase without the cast logo. Models were differentiated through identification plates on either side of the upper crankcase. The earliest examples of these were without a black background. Instead of the earlier pressed-steel sump cover, the /5 had a cast-aluminum cover, retained by 14 bolts, rather than 12. The aluminum housing for the timing chain was two-piece and smooth cast, without any air vents.

/5 Engine Specifications

Model	Bore (mm)	Stroke (mm)	Capacity (cc)	Compression Ratio	Horsepower DIN/SAE
R50/5	67	70.6	498	8.6:1	32@6400 rpm 36@6600 rpm
R60/5	73.5	70.6	599	9.2:1	40@6400 rpm 46@6600 rpm
R75/5	82	70.6	745	9.0:1	50@6200 rpm 57@6400 rpm

/5-Series Chassis Numbers

Type	Numbers	Model	Production Dates
R50/5	2900001 – 2903623	–71	09/69-08/71
	2903624 – 2907865	1972–73	09/71–08/73
R60/5	2930001 – 2938704	1970–71	09/69–08/71
	2938705 – 2952721	1972—73	09/71–08/73
R75/5	2970001 – 2982737	1970–71	09/69–08/71
	2982738 – 3000000	1972	09/71–08/73
	4000001 – 4008371	1973	

With the camshaft underneath the crankshaft and the pushrod tubes below the cylinders, the /5 engine looked quite different from the earlier /2 engine. The alternator cover was smooth on the /5.

Crankshaft and Connecting Rods

To overcome crankshaft flex as horsepower levels increased, while maintaining a design without a center main bearing, the crankshaft was now a one-piece drop-forged steel type. Rigidity was achieved by increasing the main-bearing journal diameter to 60 mm (from 35 mm on the R69S), with three-layer (bronze, tin, and indium) plain bearings shared with the newly developed six-cylinder M06* 2,500-cc BMW car engine. These bearings were pressed into a die-forged alloy bearing bush inserted in the front and rear of the crankcase.

BMW increased the big-end journal diameter (to 48 mm) and used two-piece, die-forged steel con rods (with a 22-mm off-center wrist pin). The con rods, also shared with the M06* six-cylinder car engine, ran in three-layer plain bearings, while the wrist pins ran in bronze bushes. With an eye-to-eye length of 5.265 inches (135 mm), the stroke-to-con-rod length ratio was 1.91:1, close to the optimum 2:1. An automotive-type flywheel, lighter than the one on its predecessor, bolted on the end of the crankshaft, and included a ring gear for the electric start.

Pistons and Rings

BMW fitted three-ring convex, rising-oval, forged-aluminum pistons to the /5. These were almost flat topped, with very little valve cutaway. The top compression ring was hard-chrome-plated and quite thin to avoid flutter and loss of compression at higher rpm. The second ring was an L-shaped Dykes pattern compression ring. The bottom ring was an oil-scraper ring. Higher compression competition pistons were also available for the R75/5.

Cylinders

Instead of the cast-iron cylinders used previously, BMW gave the /5 aluminum cylinders with cast-iron sleeves. The sleeves, molecularly bonded to the cylinders through a process known as Al-Fin, provided the benefit of less weight, with improved heat dissipation. Because of the more uniform expansion rates between the piston and cylinder, closer tolerances were specified (0.0035–0.0045 mm). Two pushrod tubes were pressed into the bottom of the cylinder, also providing an oil return to the crankcase. The cylinder base gasket was aluminum fiber, and the cylinder head gasket was metal and asbestos.

Cylinder Head

There was a new cylinder head design for the /5, with the two overhead valves now located with a shallower 65-degree included angle. The finned cylinder head was constructed of aluminum alloy, with shrunk-in valve seats of fine pearlitic gray iron for the intake and high-alloy gray iron for the exhaust.

Each version of the /5 came with different valve sizes, the R75/5 having valves with 42-mm intake and 38-mm exhaust, both 98 mm long. The R60/5 valves were 38-mm inlet (98.5 mm long) and 34-mm exhaust (97.5 mm long), with the R50/5 receiving 34-mm intakes (103 mm long) and 32-mm exhausts (102.5 mm long). All valve stems were hard-chrome-plated and 8 mm in diameter, while the exhaust valves had a heat-conductive, ferrite stem, and an austenitic head. The valves were actuated through 22-mm hardened followers, pushrods, and rocker arms, with the pushrod having a similar coefficient of expansion to the cylinder to maintain a consistent valve clearance. The valve springs were a single-coil type, and the valve guides were 54 mm long.

Intake manifolds were threaded, 26 mm in diameter for the R50/5 and R60/5, and 36 mm in diameter for the R75/5. The R75/5 manifold was 30 mm long, but this was later reduced to 25 mm. Four 10x275-mm studs fastened the cylinder head to the crankcase. Two additional bolts (10x30 mm and 10x50 mm) through the rocker-arm blocks and cylinder head fastened both to the cylinder. Rocker arms pivoted on 18-mm floating bronze bushings. The rocker arm ratio was 1:1.39.

Camshaft and Camshaft Drive

The case-hardened die-cast camshaft ran directly in the crankcase at the rear, and in a flanged aluminum bearing support at the front. The camshaft was phosphated for lower friction, and a rotor for the Eaton oil pump was incorporated at the rear of the camshaft. Located on the front of the camshaft were the ignition advance unit and the tachometer drive gear. While the R50/5 and R60/5 shared the same camshaft, the R75/5 used a sporting camshaft with more overlap and a 110-degree lobe center (compared to the 90-degree lobe center for the R50 and R60/5). The R75/5 camshaft also provided 0.2634 inches (6.756 mm) of valve lift, compared to 0.2417 inches (6.198 mm) for the R50/5 and R60/5 camshaft.

Instead of the previous helical gear camshaft drive, the /5 had a new duplex-chain camshaft drive, similar to that on the overhead camshaft BMW car engines. The 50-link double-roller 3/8x7/32-inch chain incorporated an automatic leaf-spring tensioner, and the lower sprocket ran in a 35x62x9-mm bearing in the housing. A 5x6.5-mm Woodruff key located the sprocket on the camshaft.

Lubrication System

All the plain bearings inside the engine required copious amounts of filtered high-pressure oil for lubrication, and this was supplied by the Eaton hypo trochoidal pump. Essentially a four-bladed impeller revolving inside a five-chamfered housing, it was capable of delivering 370 gallons (1,400 liters) per hour at 6,000 rpm. On the early /5, a very small 2.5x3.7-mm Woodruff key connected the inner rotor to the camshaft. The oil pump sucked oil from the oil pan through a suction bell with a perforated screen, and pumped it through the main

/5 Valve Timing (2 mm valve clearance, ± 2.5 degrees)

Model	Intake opening	Intake closing	Exhaust opening	Exhaust closing
R50/5, R60/5	40° BTDC	40° ABDC	40° BBDC	40° ATDC
R75/5	10° BTDC	50° ABDC	50° BBDC	10° ATDC

Bing slide-type carburetors were fitted to the R50/5 and R60/5, with float bowl ticklers instead of a choke. The silver intake tubes indicate this is a 1970–71 model.

On the R75/5 there were twin Bing CV carburetors. This type of carburetor would be a feature of nearly every later BMW air-cooled twin through 1996.

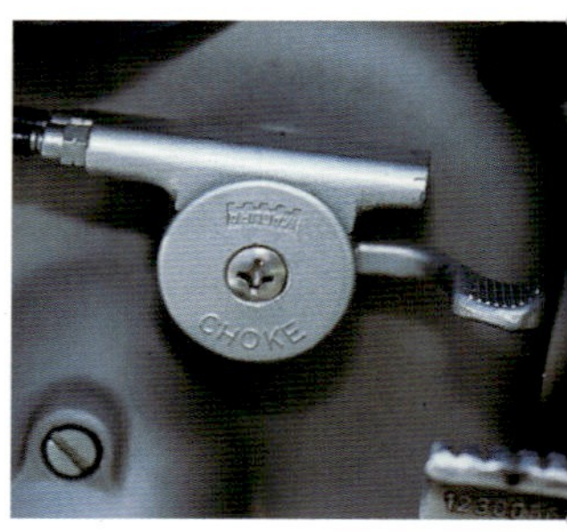

The R75/5 had a Magura choke lever, mounted on the air filter housing.

Distinctive chrome-plated cigar-style mufflers were a feature of the /5. This is a 1973 R75/5.

R75/5, R60/5, R50/5 Carburetors

	R50/5	R60/5	R75/5
Left Carburetor	Bing 1/26/113	Bing 1/26/111	Bing 64/32/3 (64/32/9 from 1971)
Right Carburetor	Bing 1/26/114	Bing 1/26/112	Bing 64/32/4 (64/32/10 from 1971)
Main Jet	135	140	135
Needle Jet	2.68	2.68	2.73 (2.70)
Jet Needle No.	46-234	46-234	46-241
Needle Position	3	2	3
Idle Jet	35	40	44-950

lubricating passages into the automotive-type disposable full-flow oil filter.

Oil was then pressure-fed to passages in the camshaft-bearing flange and the main-bearing cover, through the left side of the crankcase to the rear main bearing. It then went upward through the two upper through-bolt holes in the cylinder to the tappet-bearing blocks and shafts to lubricate the valve mechanism. The connecting rods were lubricated through holes in the crankshaft, receiving their oil from the annular groove of the front or rear main-bearing sleeve. The rear camshaft bearing was lubricated directly by the oil pump. The timing chain was splash-lubricated from the sump.

A venting dome on top of the crankcase separated the oil mist from crankcase air through a check-ball valve. This was then fed back into the intake. Undoubtedly, the efficiency of this lubrication system contributed to the outstanding reliability of the M04* engine throughout its long production lifespan.

Carburetors and Air Filtration

BMW designed an all-new air intake system for the /5. Rather than an air filter situated in a separate housing above the transmission, the /5 air filter was inside the engine cases, also at the rear above the gearbox. At the top of the housing, underneath the fuel tank, was a rear-facing air intake grill. As the air intake faced rearward, there was no ram air effect but the air filter volume was 60 percent larger than that of the R69S. A small amount of air went to cool the electrical components on the front of the engine before the filtered air entered a common chamber under the large Micro-Star disposable paper air filter element. Air then proceeded to two individual carburetor ducts. While this convoluted intake system didn't contribute to horsepower, it successfully quelled intake noise and provided excellent air filtration.

The R50/5 and R60/5 were fitted with Bing 26-mm concentric carburetors, and the R75/5 with Bing 32-mm constant-velocity (CV)-type carburetors. The R75 carburetors were also attached to the cylinder heads through short rubber sleeves and 52-mm-diameter clamps to isolate vibration. The concentric carburetors included an accelerator pump and an enriching float plunger instead of a choke. The CV carburetors included a cable-operated choke with the Magura lever positioned on the left side of the air filter housing. Unfortunately, the neoprene diaphragms in the CV carbs were thin and could rupture. This was modified for 1971. The intake tubes were silver on 1970–71 versions.

Exhaust System

All /5s shared the chrome-plated steel 38x1.5-mm exhaust headers and distinctive 100-mm-diameter cigar-shaped muffler. This large-capacity exhaust system included a cross-over pipe in front of the engine and was designed to minimize backpressure over a wide rpm range, accentuating quietness over performance.

Electrical, Charging, and Ignition Systems

At the center of the more modern 12-volt electrical system of the /5 series was an automotive-type three-phase alternator located on the end of the crankshaft. Designed by BMW and built by Bosch, this G1 14V 13A19 alternator provided only 180 watts and a maximum current of 13 amps. A diode plate mounted above the alternator rectified the alternator's output to direct current, and a Bosch AD 1/14V regulator controlled the voltage. A small Varta 15-Ah battery completed the electrical system.

The first modification to the /5 electrical system came during the autumn of 1970 (from R50/5 number 2901772, R60/5 number 2931336, and R75/5 number 2971545) when BMW began fitting a new, more flexible battery cable. At about the same time, an improved alternator rotor was introduced (from R50/5 number 2901772, R60/5 number 2932606, and R75/5 number 2973649).

A single set of breaker points, operated by the ignition cam on the end of the camshaft, triggered the /5's battery-and-coil ignition system. The ignition also included a Bosch centrifugal ignition advance unit, which began advancing the ignition at 800 rpm and reached full advance at approximately 2,500 rpm. Twin Bosch 6-volt coils were mounted in series. The high-tension leads were 21.7 inches (550 mm) long, with metal-shrouded Bosch or Beru resistor-type spark plug caps. The spark plugs were Bosch W230 T1 or Beru 230/14/3A for the R50/5 and R60/5 and Bosch W200 T30, Champion N7Y, or Beru 200/14/3A for the R75/5.

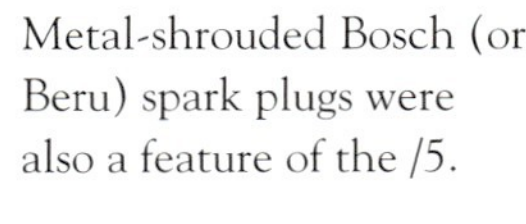
Metal-shrouded Bosch (or Beru) spark plugs were also a feature of the /5.

Starting System

Electric start was standard on the R75/5 and R60/5 but optional on the R50/5. The system was operated by a push-button on the right handlebar and consisted of a Bosch DF 12V .5-horsepower series-wound electric starter motor mounted at the top of the crankcase and a transistor-controlled relay, both hidden underneath a removable alloy cover. All /5s still had the traditional kickstart incorporated at the back of the gearbox connected to the input shaft.

Despite the small battery, electric starting on the /5s was generally reliable. The system came at a weight penalty of around 50 pounds (23 kilograms). Some early /5s came with faulty solenoids that would cause the starter to engage while the engine was running, but this was soon rectified.

Clutch

A 180-mm single-disc dry clutch connected the crankshaft and the transmission input shaft, with a diaphragm spring compressing a pressure plate and bonded friction lining clutch plate. The lighter R50/5 and R60/5 spring was 2.4 mm thick and 17.5 mm high, while the stronger R75/5 spring was 2.6 mm thick and 19.0 mm high. A diaphragm was spot-welded to the pressure plate between the flywheel and pressure ring, allowing the pressure plate to move axially, and to transmit some engine torque. The 6-mm clutch plate was mounted on the splines of the transmission input shaft and was disengaged by a pushrod inside the input shaft, activated by a lever at the back of the transmission.

BMW equipped the /5 with both an electric starter and a traditional kickstart lever behind the gearbox.

Gearbox

Like the /5 boxer engine, the /5's gearbox carried the internal designation Type 246. It was a three-shaft four-speed transmission mounted directly to the engine housing. The three shafts were the input shaft, countershaft, and output shaft. The countershaft and output shafts incorporated four gears, each in constant mesh, with a spring-and-cam shock absorber also on the output shaft. All timing shafts were supported in ball bearings. Although the gearbox shifted more smoothly than earlier BMW twins, it still wasn't flawless, and many modifications were made over the next

/5 Transmission Ratios

First Gear	3.896:1
Second Gear	2.578:1
Third Gear	1.875:1
Fourth Gear	1.50:1

/5 Final Drive Ratios

	Number of Teeth	Ratio
R50/5	9:32	1:3.56
R60/5	11:37	1:3.36
R75/5 (1970)	11:32	1:2.91
R75/5 (1971–73)	10:32	1:3.2

Like the /2, the /5 incorporated the driveshaft inside the right side of the swingarm. This is a late-1971 R60/5, number 2 938 848, ostensibly for the 1972 model year but still with many 1971 components.

The leading-axle telescopic front fork fitted to the /5 came from the /2 U.S. models of 1967–69. The outside of the front brake hub was also chrome plated.

few years. As an option, there was also a close-ratio competition gearbox.

Final Drive

Drive from the gearbox was through an enclosed driveshaft running in an oil bath in the right side of the swingarm. The driveshaft assembly featured a needle-bearing universal joint at the gearbox end, bolted to a drive flange mounted to the taper of the transmission output shaft. On the rear of the driveshaft was a troublesome, internally splined 1:6 coupling (to facilitate wheel removal). Rear drive was through a set of Klingelnberg Palloid helical-tooth spiral bevel gears. This system was already well proven on the /2 series. To provide the optimum performance, each version of the /5 received a different set of final drive ratios.

Frame and Swingarm

The chassis for the new series, also designated 246, centered on a new, lighter, two-piece frame. For the first time for a BMW standard model, there was no provision for attaching a sidecar—the lugs were omitted on the new frame, as they had been on earlier U.S. models. The frame was constructed of variable section conical tubing that included changes in taper and ovality in accordance with the anticipated stress.

The 45x3-mm-diameter dual-walled backbone was attached to double loops that varied from 28x1.5 mm to 32x3 mm in diameter. The frame was argon welded and weighed 28.6 pounds (13 kilograms). The 46x4.5-mm-diameter steering head was braced with 4-mm gussets that permitted longitudinal elasticity without affecting torsional rigidity, and the tunnel for the fuel tank was very shallow. The light triangular rear subframe bolted to the main frame with four 8-mm bolts. Two bolts fastened the engine to the frame. The strength of the structure was questioned, but the frame remained essentially unchanged through the end of Type 246 production in 1996.

Designer von der Marwitz was convinced too much frame stiffness was detrimental for a street motorcycle, so he designed in what some feel to have been too much flex. The resulting stability problems were overcome through fitting tires with stiffer sidewalls. The short swingarm also impeded stability, and this was lengthened in 1973. The swingarm pivoted in the frame on adjustable tapered roller bearings.

Unlike earlier /2 twins with a removable aluminum vehicle identification number (VIN) plate attached to the steering head, the /5 came with a paper VIN identification. The frame number was stamped to the right of the steering head.

Suspension

The /5 used the same telescopic fork manufactured by Sachs (to BMW specifications) that had been used on the U.S. models in 1967. On the /5, however, the fork pivoted on two tapered roller bearings, instead of loose ball bearings, in the steering head. Fork tubes were 36 mm in diameter and hard chromed. Fork travel was 8.2 inches (208 mm).

The triple clamp consisted of a steel upper fork yoke and a forged-aluminum lower yoke. Trail was 3.62 inches (93 mm). A 13-rib rubber gaiter protected the fork tubes from stone damage, and a tubular steel brace provided additional rigidity. All the /5s had a friction steering damper, with a knob adjuster on top of the upper fork yoke, with a more effective hydraulic steering damper available as an option.

The early forks suffered from stiction caused by the one-piece bushing held by a snap ring inside the fork tubes, but this was modified in 1972. With their soft fork springs, they also dived under braking, and a stiffer fork spring and damping ring were offered as an option.

At the rear, twin 12.3-inch (316-mm) Boge shock absorbers provided 4.92 inches (125 mm) of spring travel. An alloy cover hid springs on these shocks. Spring preload was adjusted by means of a lever at the bottom of the shock absorber. The

All /5s were fitted with the protective fork gaiters and a chrome-plated steel fender brace.

A black knob operated the friction damper on the /5. The flex-prone pressed-steel upper triple clamp was the weak link in the fork assembly.

The Boge shock absorbers on the /5 had aluminum covers and black springs.

A single cable operated the new double-leading-shoe front brake. The spokes were also a new type for the /5.

Both the front and rear brakes featured chrome-plated covers on the left side.

springs were black, and the shock absorber pressure was 240–310 Kilo-Pascal.

Wheels, Tires, and Brakes

High-quality aluminum wheel rims graced the /5, a 1.85Bx19-inch on the front and 1.85Bx18-inch on the rear. Forty 4-mm spokes laced each rim to its hub, and these spokes were of a new design, more reliable than those on the /2, which sometimes failed as a result of the spoke head breaking off. This spoke type was changed again for the 1973 model year.

Instead of a rim lock to prevent the tire bead leaving the rim if the tire deflated, BMW wheel rims were stamped with five dents opposite the valve stem. The five dents prevented the tire bead from moving into the center well, allowing the other side to climb off the rim. The wheel bearings were a sealed taper roller type, and the front axle was 14 mm. Because of problems with stability on early /5 models, specific Continental or Metzeler tires were specified, a rib 3.25x19-inch on the front and 4.00x18-inch Universal on the rear.

Both front and rear hubs were fitted with new, more rigid brake drums with deep stiffening and cooling ridges in the alloy housing. The front brake was a 200x30-mm Duplex (double leading shoe), with a 200x30-mm Simplex (single leading shoe) on the rear. Both brakes also featured chrome-plated covers on the left side.

Although the /5 shoes were narrower than those of the /2, the new BMW's brakes were considerably more effective, due to the new bonded brake linings developed for Porsche cars earlier in the 1960s. Rather than an adjustable rod between

Below left: High-quality Magura levers and a cam-and-chain throttle distinguished the /5.

Below: The aluminum Magura clutch lever pivoted on Teflon bushings.

the two front brake pivot arms, with both arms pulling in the same direction, the single brake cable attached directly to the arms, moving them together when the front brake lever was pulled. The system worked well, and when the front brake was properly adjusted, it was perfectly adequate. Rear brake actuation was by a rod.

The large fuel tank of 1970–71 /5s featured hand-painted pinstripes and rubber kneepads.

The /5 was the final BMW motorcycle to include enamel tank emblems.

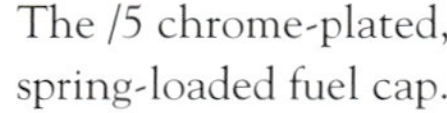

The /5 chrome-plated, spring-loaded fuel cap.

This lockable cap was available as an option.

Handlebars, Levers, and Mirrors

Two types of chrome-plated tubular steel handlebars were initially available for the /5: a 23.6-inch (600-mm) and optional, higher 26.8-inch (680-mm) handlebar. U.S. models had the higher and wider handlebars. The handlebars attached to the top fork crown with two-piece aluminum risers similar to those of the 1967–69 U.S. telescopic fork R50, R60, and R69.

The handlebar controls on the /5s were also similar to the final /2 controls, and were of exceptionally high quality, featuring Magura forged aluminum levers with finger indentations. Each lever had Teflon bushings at the pivots, with spring washers between the lever and body to ensure a smooth action.

The throttle control incorporated a cam and chain, similar in design to the previous R50/R60/R69 throttle, but providing a quicker and more progressive action. Unlike the earlier twins, the /5s were fitted with a rubber boot where the cables entered the throttle.

Generally only one handlebar-mounted rear vision mirror was fitted to the /5s, although both lever assemblies had mirror mounts. The chrome-plated round mirrors screwed into threaded holes in the lever mounts. Both short- and long-stemmed mirrors were specified, the short-stemmed mirrors intended for the higher U.S. handlebars. It appears there was little consistency in what was fitted, however, and neither type of mirror was very satisfactory, especially above 70 miles per hour (113 kilometers per hour).

Fuel Tank and Fenders

The large 6.35-gallon (22-liter) fuel tank was rubber mounted with a single rubber pad at the front and two rubber blocks at the rear. It was retained by two wing nuts at the rear. The paint quality was extremely high, with fastidiously accurate hand-painted pinstripes. The tank incorporated rubber kneepads on each side, and the traditional fired cloisonné enamel BMW emblems with rubber washers were screwed into the tank with two 4x8-mm oval-headed screws. There was a nonlockable fuel filler cap, although a locking filler cap was an option. Also optional was a fuel tank that incorporated a lockable toolbox in the top, similar to that of some earlier BMW motorcycles.

The fuel tank was constructed in two sections to clear the frame backbone, so BMW added a fuel petcock on each side. These screwed directly into the tank, and one-piece metal Everbest taps were fitted through the /6 series. After 1973, Karcoma or Germa fuel petcocks were also fitted, depending on supply at the time of manufacture. These were all interchangeable, but the Everbest wasn't easily rebuilt, and used unreliable cork seals that could block the fuel flow.

BMW is justly famous for its paint and striping and both on the /5 were of exceptional quality.

Unlike the earlier /2, the /5 was equipped with two Everbest fuel taps.

Initially only black (with white pinstripes), metallic silver (with blue pinstripes), and white (with black pinstripes) /5s were produced, although nearly all /5s for the United States were black in 1970 and 1971.

The fenders on /5s were made of fiberglass, in a move to reduce weight, and were painted to match the fuel tank, with pinstripes. Generally the pinstripe color matched that of the fuel tank, but not always, and this inconsistency accentuated the handcrafted aspect of the /5.

Seat, Badges, and Frame Fittings

The dual Denfeld seat hinged from the right, revealing a storage tray. Unlike the ignition, the seat was lockable, using the same Neiman key as the steering lock. The chrome passenger grab rail was two-piece, one on each side, and there was no model identification badge on the rear of the seat. A solo seat with lockable rear compartment was an option.

Denfeld also made the round footpeg rubbers. A centerstand and sidestand were both standard equipment. The sidestand was manually retractable on 1970 and 1971 /5s. To help the rider lift the bike up and back onto its centerstand, BMW added a chrome-plated lifting handle near the seat lock. To protect the engine in a tip-over, a factory engine protection bar was available as an option. Other options included a luggage rack, leather saddlebags, hard plastic bags, and a black rear mudflap with a BMW logo.

Toolkit and Handbook

Each /5 came with a model-specific rider's handbook, in a plastic envelope, and the usual comprehensive 22-piece (later 26-piece) BMW toolkit, with embroidered towel, tire repair kit, and tire pump. The tire pump was located under the seat, on the left of the rear subframe. An even more comprehensive 33-piece toolkit was available as an option through 1984.

ELECTRICS, CONTROLS, AND INSTRUMENTS

Switchgear and Horn

On the left handlebar was a three-way Hella horn/high-beam and headlight flasher switch, with the turn signals and starter on the right. The live headlamp flasher was unfused, and could cause a fire in extreme circumstances. The hard rubber handgrips were made by Magura.

The /5 carried over one odd relic of the past: the plunger switch in the headlight that operated the ignition and lights. Vehicle security was marginal, as the same plunger would operate the switch on any /5, or indeed any BMW motorcycle from the 1936 R5 and R12. Not really an ignition key but more of a kill switch in reverse, it did have its advantages, as it could be operated with gloves, and it easily snapped into position. The plunger receptacle had a spring-loaded cover that provided effective water protection.

A Bosch 0320 123013 horn was fitted on 1970 models, and a heavy-duty low-tone horn was optional.

Instruments

Along with the plunger ignition key, the /5 kept one other relic of past BMWs: the instrument cluster incorporated in the headlamp. Covered under a 3-inch (76-mm) circle of glass, the cluster consisted of a mechanical speedometer and tachometer, along with warning lights for high beam (blue), neutral (green), oil pressure (orange), and alternator (red). There was an odometer but no room for a trip meter. The MotoMeter instruments featured white numbers on a black background, but the numbers were quite small and difficult to read, not only while riding. The speedometer read from 10–120 miles per hour (or 20–200 kilometers per hour), and the

DIMENSIONS, WEIGHTS, AND PERFORMANCE

	R50/5	R60/5	R75/5
Overall width	29.1 inches	29.1 inches	29.1 inches
Saddle height	33.5 inches	33.5 inches	33.5 inches
Overall length	82.7 inches	82.7 inches	82.7 inches
Overall length (1973)	84.6 inches	84.6 inches	84.6 inches
Wheelbase	54.53 inches	54.53 inches	54.53 inches
Wheelbase (1973)	56.5 inches	56.5 inches	56.5 inches
Weight including oil but without fuel	412 lbs	423 lbs	423 lbs
Weight including oil and fuel	452 lbs	463 lbs	463 lbs
Top speed	98 mph	104 mph	110 mph
Standing 1/4 mile	17.2 seconds	15.8 seconds	14.6 seconds

tachometer to 8,000 rpm, with the redline at 6,800 rpm. Some examples didn't include a redline. The instruments differed for the various models of the /5 because the speedometer drive was from the gearbox, and the final drive ratios differed. Each speedometer was matched for a specific final drive ratio. If not properly routed, the clutch, choke, and throttle cables could also obscure the tachometer face, a problem that was more common with the higher U.S. handlebars.

Headlamp, Taillight, and Turn Signals

The Bosch 0 303 550 002 headlamp was a 6-inch (160-mm) 45/40-watt unit, inserted in a metal shell. There was also an optional H4 headlamp conversion. The taillight was a rectangular Hella, with U.S. models receiving a specific taillight lens that differed from European versions in that there was no circle in the center. The rectangular turn signals had aluminum bodies, and U.S. models for 1970 and 1971 featured reflectors on the front and rear turn signals.

1971 R75/5, R60/5, and R50/5

BMW made only a few changes to the /5 series after the first model year. New for 1971 was a fifth

The 1970 and 1971 /5s included twin passenger grab rails on each side of the seat, but had no sidecovers to hide the battery.

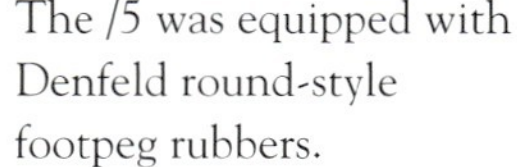

The /5 was equipped with Denfeld round-style footpeg rubbers.

BMW equipped its air-cooled twins with a tire pump, mounted on the left of the rear subframe on twin-shock-absorber models.

The Hella handlebar switches were idiosyncratic, and not particularly ergonomic in design.

Also eccentric was the plunger ignition switch inherited from the /2.

Early /5s featured a round Bosch horn with a chrome center section.

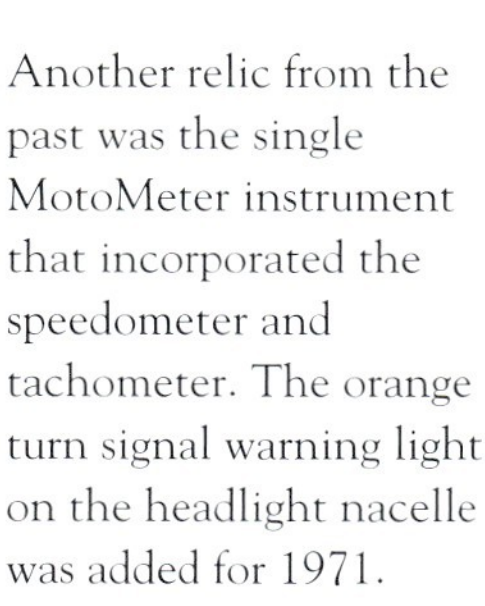

Another relic from the past was the single MotoMeter instrument that incorporated the speedometer and tachometer. The orange turn signal warning light on the headlight nacelle was added for 1971.

warning light, a single indicator light for the turn signals added to the left of the ignition switch in the headlight. This was usually green, but orange on some versions.

During the summer of 1971, from R75/5 number 2977320, BMW began to fit new 32-mm Bing vacuum carburetors, along with a new Magura choke-lever assembly with stronger cables. The new carburetors featured a revised throttle slide with a greater wall clearance, different needle jet, stronger neoprene diaphragm, and a domed carburetor cover, resulting in an improved idle. The carburetor types were now Bing 64/32/9 and 64/32/10.

In an effort to improve acceleration, BMW lowered the high R75/5 final drive ratio to 1:3.2 (10:32), after number 2973204. The final drive ratios for the R50/5 and R60/5 were unchanged.

From R50/5 number 2901787, R60/5 number 2932689, and R75/5 number 9273307, there was a new centrifugal advance unit. This provided maximum advance at 3,000 rpm. In the spring of 1971 (from R50/5 number 2902093, R60/5 number 2933525, and R75/5 number 2975253), the battery carrier was modified to include five rubber buffers.

1972 R75/5, R60/5, and R50/5

The /5 had many updates for the 1972 model year. Most controversial was the smaller fuel tank with chrome panels, known later as the "toaster" because of its similarity to the kitchen appliance. The "toaster" ran from September 1971 (R50/5 number 2903624, R60/5 number 2938705, R75/5 number 2982741), to August 1972 (R50/5 number 2905616, R60/5 number 2945288, R75/5 number 2994267). The radical styling of the "toaster" wasn't universally accepted, and it wasn't offered for 1973.

Engine

Changes to the engine were again minimal, but from February 1972 there was a stronger crankshaft with new bearing shells (from R50/5 number 2904190, R60/5 number 2940740, and R75/5 number 2985208). The engine housing was also modified, and this would run through the 1976 model year. Soon afterward there were new rocker shaft supporting brackets and hardened steel shims to reduce noise (from R50/5 number 2904721, R60/5 number 2942632, and R75/5 number 2989472). The R75/5 from number 2992320 also received vacuum ports on the carburetors. Later in the 1972 production run and continuing for 1973 and the /6 of 1974, the carburetor air intakes on some R75/5s were black instead of silver. These black intakes were a precursor for the 1973 model year, providing more legroom, but only a few 1972 R75/5s had them.

The aluminum model identification badges on the engine cases were now with a black background. Also new were slightly thinner (38x1-mm) exhaust header pipes, and some of the final U.S. examples featured additional vented heat shields over the header pipes.

Fuel Tank, Side Panels, and Seat

The /5 styling makeover for 1972 centered on a new 4.6-gallon (17-liter) fuel tank, with garish chrome-plated side panels and matching chrome-plated side covers to hide the battery. The tank incorporated three painted stripes, and the side panels had four stripes. A wider selection of colors was also available for 1972: Monza metallic blue (with white pinstripes), metallic curry gold (with black stripes), red (with white stripes), and green metallic (with white stripes). Most U.S. 1972 models were black, blue, or silver, with black or blue stripes on the chromed panels. It appears there was inconsistency as to the color of these stripes, but they were intended to match the tank color.

Along with the smaller fuel tank, BMW gave the toaster /5s a new seat, with a single handrail running across and behind the passenger, a black highlighted emblem on the rear of the saddle, a white bead following the line of the handrail, and longitudinal pleating on the upholstery.

Handlebars, Mirrors, Reflectors, Horn, and Sidestand

Along with slightly wider 25-inch (650-mm) handlebars, many examples of the 1972 /5 had two mirrors, although this wasn't universal. U.S. models still had the higher 27-inch (680-mm) handlebar. U.S. and European versions now shared the same turn signals, with the large round U.S.-required reflectors located on the headlight brackets at the front and license plate bracket at the rear. There were new headlight brackets for 1972, and many 1972 models had a Hella B31 horn. This large round horn had a chrome-plated grill, as did the equivalent Bosch horn this year. The 1972 /5 also came with an automatically retracting sidestand.

Suspension

One of the more significant improvements for 1972 was to the front fork, to reduce stiction. A three-piece floating damper nozzle replaced the earlier fixed bushing, the aluminum center damper ring supported by two outer threaded rings that allowed the piston to move more freely. While the shock absorbers were unchanged, the springs were now chrome-plated. This continued on 1973 versions.

The 6½-inch 12-volt Bosch headlight was only 45 watts but provided a vast improvement over that of the earlier /2.

A European-specification taillight, with a large circle in the center.

The U.S taillight lens differed from the European lens.

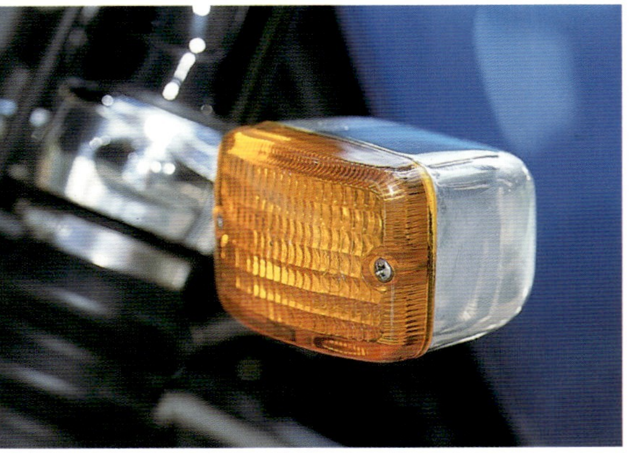

The rectangular Hella turn-signals featured aluminum bodies.

Plain polished aluminum model emblems on the engine also distinguished 1970 and 1971 versions.

For 1972 the /5 received controversial chrome-plated panels in the smaller fuel tank, earning the nickname the "toaster."

Along with the chrome tank panels were chrome-plated battery covers. The grills were painted to match the tank and fenders.

The 1972 and 1973 seats featured larger passenger grab handles and a model emblem at the rear.

Wheels

Although the tire sizes remained unchanged, from October 1971 all /5s (from R50/5 number 2903756, R60/5 number 2939207, and R75/5 number 2983280) received a wider WM3 2.15Bx18-inch rear wheel rim.

1973 R75/5, R60/5, and R50/5

BMW made a number of changes to the /5 series frame and cycle parts for 1973. The most noticeable was the longer swingarm, included from January 1973. From June 1973, the R75/5 also incorporated a spacer tube at the rear crankcase mount, which continued on all later models from the /6 onward. In addition to the normal U.S.-specification machines imported by Butler and Smith, a number of European-specification /5s from the Italian distributor ended up in the United States toward the end of 1973. These bikes had different reflectors, with the rear reflectors glued to the fender, as the license plate bracket was flat.

Engine

The /5 engines got a new inner rotor for the oil pump, with a larger 3.0x5.0-mm Woodruff key connecting it to the camshaft. The Woodruff key for the camshaft drive sprocket was also reduced to the same 3.0x5.0 mm, so there was a new camshaft. There was another centrifugal advance unit, fitted from November 1972 (from R50/5 number 2905857, R60/5 number 2946096, and R75/5 number 2996220). Ignition advance commenced at a later 1,550 rpm, with full advance at 3,000 rpm.

Chassis

As the radical styling of 1972 wasn't universally accepted, BMW reprised traditional conservative styling for 1973. Standard again was the 6.25-gallon (24-liter) tank with rubber kneepads, while the smaller 4.4-gallon (17-liter) tank was optional, also with rubber pads rather than the previous chrome-plated panels. The side battery covers were also optional, but these were now painted black or blue rather than chrome plated.

Also new for 1973 was a revised top throttle cam cover, and U.S. examples got a new Hella taillight lens. Soon after 1973 model year production commenced—from October 1972 (R50/5 number 2905828, R60/5 number 2946037, R75/5 number 2995073), the adjuster for the steering head bearing was changed from a round indented nut to a large hexagonal nut.

The longer swingarm was fitted after R50/5 number 2906304, R60/5 number 2947966, and R75/5 number 2997986. The splined coupling ratio was now 1:7. The new swingarm lengthened the wheelbase 1.97 inches (50 mm) and improved

A restored example of a 1973 R75/5 (number 4002607). This features the longer swingarm, optional larger gas tank, and battery covers. Nonstandard are the shock absorbers without spring covers, but in every other respect this is how the 1973 R75/5

stability. It was also claimed to provide increased clearance between the riders' shins and carburetors, but as the footpegs were in the same position this was achieved through the new shape of the black intakes.

On the first examples of long-wheelbase /5s the extra swingarm length was rather crudely achieved through an inserted welded sleeve, with a temporary fender mount. Eventually, a specific longer swingarm was installed, appearing on most final /5s. Accompanying the longer swingarm were a longer saddle, longer rear subframe, longer rear brake rod, and longer rear fender mounting bolts. The rear-drive oil capacity was also increased to 150 cc (from 100 cc) of SAE 90 hypoid gear oil

The long wheelbase significantly improved the straight-line stability of the /5, reducing wobbles, and it also enhanced cornering ability through better weight distribution. It also allowed more room in the frame for a larger 16-Ah battery. BMW claimed the longer swingarm provided increased clearance between the rider's shins and the carburetors, but because the footpegs were in the same position on both long- and short-swingarm /5s, the swingarm could not have provided the extra clearance. Actually, the extra legroom was provided by the reshaped intake manifolds that had been introduced on the last 1972 /5s. These manifolds were painted black.

As the appearance of the longer swingarm almost coincided with the announcement of the new /6 series, this modification was obviously intended for the new higher performance R90/6 and R90S.

Wheels

To overcome problems with the spoke heads disintegrating on the rear wheel, from September

From 1972, the horn included a chrome-plated grill.

Engine emblems from 1972 featured a black background.

1972, from R50/5 number 2905646, R60/5 number 2945366, and R75/5 number 2994445, BMW moved the rear-wheel spokes 0.58 inch (1.5 mm) to the left and began fitting spokes of a new type. The spoke now had a small shoulder that kept it from spinning if the tension was correct.

End of the Road

On July 28, 1973, only three days after the 500,000th BMW motorcycle (an R75/5) came off the production line, the last /5 left Spandau. In October 1973, the /5 was replaced by a next-generation series of BMW motorcycles—the /6 series.

Over its four-year lifespan, the /5 series more than lived up to its expectations. BMW built nearly 69,000 of the /5 series, a total that almost matched the entire production run of the R50, R60, and /2 series from 1955 through 1969. Not only did it continue the BMW motorcycle tradition of offering unparalleled touring comfort and reliability, the /5 (particularly the R75/5) also provided acceptable performance. Although the skeptics initially criticized the lighter frame design with its bolt-on rear subframe, it was soon evident that the /5 provided better handling than any previous BMW motorcycle. With this improved performance came the usual BMW high quality of manufacture and execution. Only in a few details did the /5 remain outdated. By 1973 the single-face combined speedometer and tachometer and the plunger ignition switch were decidedly old fashioned. The era of the disc brake and the closer-ratio five-speed gearboxes had arrived.

Possibly because it remained old fashioned in certain areas, the /5 has become a desirable motorcycle. There is little to complain about in the way it functions, and a /5 is as reliable as most later BMWs. The engine remains oil tight, and the four-speed gearbox is adequate, as the powerband is relatively broad. For most situations the drum brakes are also sufficient, and the long-wheelbase examples provide excellent and sure-footed handling, certainly on par with the /6 and /7 series.

Many of the features that made motorcycles of the early 1970s so appealing also characterize the /5. Many components that were metal on the /5 were changed to plastic on later models in the quest for economy. The /5 was the last BMW motorcycle with enamel tank badges, and the quality of the paint, chrome, and fittings was exceptional for a mass-produced motorcycle. It was all the small details that contributed to the /5 series' classic status as one of the more sought-after modern BMW motorcycles. Later models offer improved performance, but as production moved toward the economy of scale, much was lost in the process.

/5 Production

Model (Dates)	1969	1970	1971	1972	1973	Total
R50/5 11/69-04/73	399	2,053	1,737	2,130	1,546	7,865
R60/5 09/69-04/73	666	4,116	6,645	6,564	4,730	22,721
R75/5 10/69-08/73	540	6,118	10,390	12,428	8,894	38,370

Chapter 3

R90S (1974–76)

There are few motorcycles as handsome and purposeful as the R90S. This is the author's restored 1976 example.

While the /6 series was very much a continuation of the /5 concept, the new sporting R90S saw a significant change in direction for BMW. Not only did the R90S boast innovative styling, it provided class-leading performance. For the first and only time in its history, BMW offered a production motorcycle with performance comparable to that of any motorcycle produced in Japan, Italy, or England. The R90S was the first BMW superbike, and with it the conservative image of BMW motorcycles changed forever.

1974 R90S

The impetus for the creation of a BMW superbike apparently came from Bob Lutz, BMW's American-born sales director, reputedly also responsible for the toaster-tank /5s of 1972. Toaster styling may have received a lukewarm reception, but the R90S was an immediate success, despite its considerable $3,430 price tag. Underneath the R90S was an almost stock R90/6, but stylist Hans A. Muth created one of the most spectacular looking BMW motorcycles ever. In every respect the R90S was an aesthetic triumph.

Engine and Drivetrain

The updated M04* engine for the /6 series was known as Type 247. For it, BMW retained the essential architecture of the /5 engine but bolted a five-speed transmission to the rear of the engine housing. As the complete new transmission was

When introduced in 1973 for the 1974 model year, the smoke silver R90S created a sensation, and it is easy to see why. This unrestored 1974 example (number 4073237) is close to 100 percent original. The R90S (and /6) engine received a finned alternator cover.

R90S Chassis Numbers

Type	Numbers	Model	Production Dates
R90S	4070001 to 4080000	1974	09/73-08/74
R90S	4080001 to 4090000	1975	09/74-08/75
R90S	4090001 to 4100000	1976	09/75-08/76
R90S (United States)	4950001 to 4960000	1974	09/73-08/74
R90S (United States)	4980001 to 4990000	1975	09/74-08/75
R90S (United States)	4990001 to 4991260	1976	09/75-08/76

R90S Engine Specifications

Bore (mm)	Stroke (mm)	Capacity (cc)	Compression Ratio	Horsepower DIN/SAE
90	70.6	898	9.5:1	67@7000 rpm 75@7200 rpm

lighter than the four-speed, the complete R90S engine, with starter motor and carburetors, but without the ignition coils and intake system, weighed less than that of the R75/5, at 137.7 pounds (62.5 kilograms). The R90S engine was very similar to that of the R90/6 (covered in chapter 4), except for a higher compression ratio and larger carburetors.

Crankcase

The basic engine housing was carried over from the previous (1973 model) R75/5, but was strengthened around the front crankcase aperture. The front crankshaft bearing was now in a closed seat, and all the /6 series engines shared a new outer alternator and ignition cover. This featured five vertical ribs on the front, and three air vents on the bottom of each side. The inner camshaft drive support remained smoothly finished on the outside. There were no changes to the lubrication system, but the Eaton-type oil pump now featured a new inner rotor. The check valve for the engine breather was also modified slightly for the larger engine, with a lower spring groove. Also specific to the R90S was a black "BMW R90S" emblem, with silver and red highlights.

Crankshaft, Connecting Rods, Cylinders, and Pistons

There was a new crankshaft for the R90S, balanced for the larger, 90-mm, pistons. At the time these were among the largest-diameter pistons fitted to a production motorcycle. As the strengthened front crankcase tunnel aperture was too small to allow a large fully counterweighted crankshaft to pass through, 90 percent tungsten plugs were inserted in the crank webs to restore the balance. The counterweight diameter was reduced, but even with the smaller crank weights and tungsten plugs, the crankshaft was a very tight fit through the front crankcase opening and required tilting for removal and installation. The flywheel and thrust ring bolted to the crankshaft with 32-mm-long bolts, rather than the 24-mm-long bolts of the /5. The fins on the aluminum cylinders were painted black on the R90S, for improved heat dissipation.

Cylinder Head and Camshaft

R90S cylinder heads were little changed from those of the R75/5. BMW retained the same included valve angle and the 42-mm inlet valve, but increased the diameter of the exhaust valve to 40 mm. The exhaust valve length was still 98.8 mm, with an 8-mm stem, and the valves were now constructed of a high-tensile Nimonic steel alloy. There were shorter (48-mm) valve guides for the R90S, and the rocker arms pivoted in needle roller bearings, rather than bronze bushes, with new rocker support blocks. The R90S also had larger (38-mm) intake manifolds. The 308-degree camshaft was the same as that of the R75/5, R90/6, and R75/6, but a sporting 336-degree camshaft was available as an option.

Carburetors, Air Filtration, and Exhaust System

The R90S was fitted with the same Micro-Star dry air filter as on the R75/5, but it was housed in a new aluminum air filter housing with larger intakes.

In a departure from the traditional Bing carburetors, BMW fitted two Italian 38-mm Dell'Orto PHM concentric carburetors. These high-performance carburetors were a relatively new type, developed primarily for racing Ducatis during 1972. They incorporated an accelerator pump, and on the earliest R90Ss the carburetor bodies were smooth cast without any provision for a choke attachment. Starting enrichment was by a float depressor, similar to that on the slide Bing carburetor of the R50/5 and R60/5. These smooth-cast Dell'Orto bodies were shared with the early Ducati 750 Super Sport, and replacements are very difficult to obtain nowadays. On these very early R90Ss, the cast choke mount on the left side of the airbox housing was blanked off. It wasn't long, however, before Dell'Orto began to supply carburetors with a cast choke attachment, and most 1974 R90Ss included the choke, and Magura choke lever. The Dell'Orto carburetors of this era also featured polished aluminum float bowls and aluminum banjo fittings.

Instead of the cigar-shaped muffler of the /5, the R90S had new chrome-plated 3.39-inch (87-mm) diameter mufflers, with 38x1.5-mm header pipes. They were still extremely quiet, with a claimed noise level of 76 decibels. BMW also supplied a specific muffler only for California, Florida, and Oregon.

R90S CARBURETORS

Left Carburetor	Dell'Orto PHM 38 BS
Right Carburetor	Dell'Orto PHM 38 BD
Main Jet	155
Needle Jet	2.60
Jet Needle No.	K4
Needle Position	3
Idle Jet	60

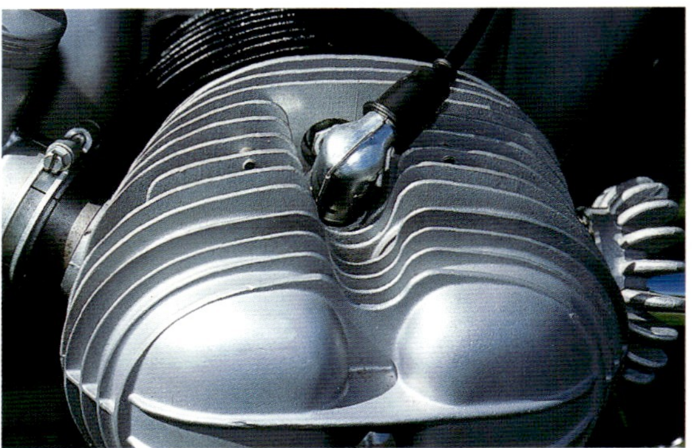

Also setting the R90S engine apart were specific model emblems on the crankcases.

The R90S also had black-painted aluminum cylinders for improved heat dissipation.

Only featured on the R90S, the 38-mm Dell'Orto carburetors contributed to the improved power and looked impressive. While the very earliest examples were without a choke, most had this choke attachment.

Only the 1974 R90S included a kickstart as standard, but it remained an option on subsequent models. Exposed fork tubes accentuated the sporting profile.

Electrical System, Alternator, Ignition, and Starting

BMW gave the R90S a new higher output three-phase Bosch alternator, a 0 120 340 003 61, 14V 17A 22/238 W. This provided an output of 240 watts, with 18 amps of current. It was smaller in outside diameter and was less powerful than the alternator of the other /6 models. The reason for the smaller alternator was to provide more clearance between the stator and alternator at higher rpm when crankshaft whip was more evident.

Other updates included a new Bosch diode board, a 25-Ah Varta battery, and a new ignition-advance unit (shared with the R90/6). Additionally, the dwell angle on the contact breaker was increased to 110 degrees (from 78 degrees). The same Bosch W200 T30 and Beru 200/12/3A spark plugs were specified for the R90S, although the Champion plugs specified were now N6Y. The spark plug caps were the same metal-shrouded Bosch or Beru units as on the /5.

Although the Bosch .5-horsepower starter motor was unchanged from that of the /5, it was activated by a new Stribel SR 9572 starter relay. A kickstart was also retained on the first-model R90Ss, although the kickstart lever was now wider, and the pedal more curved and longer. This lever was interchangeable with the earlier type.

Clutch, Gearbox, and Final Drive

The clutch for all /6s incorporated a new forged pressure ring, with ribbed supports, but the R90S also received a stronger diaphragm spring, 2.8 mm thick. The five-speed Type 247 transmission and housing was completely new, with the aluminum housing lighter and smaller than the previous four-speed housing. The casting was a high-pressure die casting, with extensive internal webbing. Still a three-shaft gearbox design, with the shafts supported in ball bearings, the five-speed shifted more smoothly than previous BMW transmissions because it included a redesigned twin-shaft ratchet gear-selector mechanism. The R90S gearbox shifted through a shorter gear lever with a less noticeable clunk than that of the R75/5. To compensate for the higher performance

R90S Transmission Ratios

First Gear	4.4:1	
Second Gear	2.86:1	
Third Gear	2.07:1	
Fourth Gear	1.67:1	
Fifth Gear	1.50:1	
Final Drive Ratio	**Number of Teeth**	**Ratio**
Stock	11:33	1:3.0

and improved aerodynamics, the R90S had a higher final drive ratio than other /6s. Four other final drive ratios were available as an option, from 1:3.36 to 1:2.91.

CYCLE PARTS

Frame and Swingarm

Designated Type 247, the black-painted R90S frame was a development of that of the R75/5. It was built of 1-5/16-inch outer diameter steel tubing, with an internal cylindrical tube, with some additional gussets, specifically around the steering head. The bolt-on rear subframe was new. The new frame was fitted with the longer swingarm of the 1973 model /5, with a 1:7 spline coupling. The new frame stretched the wheelbase out a full 3.15 inches (80 mm) from that of the first /5 of 1969.

Suspension

The Fichtel & Sachs leading axle 36-mm telescopic fork was internally identical to that of the 1973 R75/5 (providing the same 8.11 inches of travel), except for a steel upper triple clamp unique to the R90S, and a new lower forged aluminum triple clamp shared with other /6s. The fork springs (21.38 inches, or 567 mm), were longer than other /6s, with sporty rubber fork cups replacing fork gaiters and new lower fork legs with brake caliper mounts on both sides. Inside the fork cups were oil-soaked felt rings to maintain a smooth action. The lower fork leg crush washer was now 42x49 mm, instead of the 45x52 mm of the /5. U.S.-specification versions had a rectangular reflector screwed to the fender mounts; reflectors were not fitted to European-specification bikes. The 316-mm Boge shock absorbers were new for the R90S and /6 series, but the stroke was unchanged. The springs were now black. A stiffer spring was optional.

Wheels, Tires, and Brakes

The light alloy wheel rims were also similar to those of the 1973 /5, a 1.85x19-inch on the front, and a 2.15x18-inch on the rear. Heat-treated rims were optional. Tire sizes were the same as those of the /5, although H-rated tires were specified for the R90S. For 1974 these were generally Continental or Metzeler, and the hard compound was not really suitable for the sporting nature of the R90S. The front hub was a strong finned casting, laced to the rim by 40 4-mm straight-pull spokes. Spokes were made of stainless steel. The axle was still 14 mm on 1974 models.

New for the R90S were dual 260-mm stainless-steel front disc brakes, with black anodized floating single-piston ATE calipers. Caliper pistons were 38 mm in diameter, and an eccentric pin underneath the fork leg allowed brake-pad adjustment.

All R90Ss had dual-disc front brakes, but 1974 examples had undrilled rotors, and a smaller axle. This European-specification model is without reflectors on the fork legs.

The flexible rubber brake hoses contributed to the soft feel of the front braking system.

Low sporting handlebars, /5 switches, and an adjustable steering damper distinguished the cockpit of the 1974 R90S. These early instruments are missing their aluminum surrounds but are otherwise correct. The steel upper triple clamp was also specific for the R90S.

The fuel tank was a masterful piece, possessing graceful lines and a useful capacity, without excessive width.

The 15.87-mm ATE master cylinder, with round fluid reservoir, was located underneath the fuel tank, and rather crudely attached to the top frame tube with a hose clamp. A Bowden cable connected the master cylinder to the handlebar-mounted brake lever. Early in the production run, BMW switched to a thinner, more square-shaped reservoir for the master cylinder. This provided more clearance between the master cylinder and the bottom of the fuel tank.

The brake lines consisted of metal tubes at either end of the 27-inch flexible rubber brake hose, connecting to the brake caliper and master cylinder. U.S. models had different-specification brake hoses.

While the rear brake remained a 200-mm Simplex, U.S. DOT requirements for 1974 required a method for checking the condition of the brake linings without removing the wheel. To provide inspection windows, BMW left off the chrome-plated hubcap-style cover and redesigned the hub casting with stronger ribs. The linings were also colored to facilitate inspection. The brake actuation was through a rod, like the /5, and the 40 rear spokes were also the stronger straight-pull type.

Handlebars, Levers, and Mirrors

A low 23.4x0.86-inch (600x22-mm) sporting handlebar was fitted to the R90S, but the U.S. model was slightly broader than European versions while still 23.4 inches (600 mm) wide. Black highlighted aluminum brackets clamped the handlebars to the top triple clamp. The Magura clutch and brake levers were matte black, but still with incorporated finger grooves. The Magura throttle assembly was as on the /5, but as it was designed for smaller-bodied carburetors it was very slow acting with the large 38-mm Dell'Orto carburetors. Also unchanged were the Magura handgrips. The two round mirrors were black on the R90S.

Fuel Tank, Fairing, Side Panels, and Fenders

The R90S had a new steel 6.24-gallon (24-liter) fuel tank, without kneepads (although they were an option). The tank badges were now plastic, and glued into place. For 1974 the only color was silver smoke (code 561). The silver smoke was hand painted and airbrushed, with a clear lacquer over the paint. Early R90Ss had gold tape instead of the usual hand-painted pinstripes, because a suitable paint to provide a uniform finish wasn't initially available. The gold tape was also available as a spare part for the fenders. While some early examples had the earlier Everbest metal fuel petcocks, from mid-1974 most R90Ss had Karcoma or Germa petcocks (labeled in English and German). The tank was still retained at the rear by two wing nuts on early examples.

The matching handlebar-mounted fairing was fiberglass, and included plastic automotive-style padding. Not only was the quality of the fairing exceptional, but the R90S was the first mainstream motorcycle to include a fairing as standard equipment. The Plexiglas screen was attached with 10 A6x0.4x8-mm rivets.

The fenders were also fiberglass. The front was the longer of the two /6 types. The beautifully formed sidecovers were also the same as the /6 pieces, as was the rear fender. The quality of the fiberglass was unsurpassed. Instead of the external tubular steel upper brace joining the front fork legs, a pressed steel brace was incorporated underneath the fender. As with the /5, a black rear mud flap was optional.

Seat, Badges, and Frame Fittings

Part of the styling makeover for the R90S included a new Denfeld seat, with a fiberglass base and a sporting rear cowling. Underneath the hinged, lockable seat were two large storage trays, and the removable tray was different than those of the /5 and /6. At the rear was a very useful compartment. The seat included a single chrome-plated handrail. The seat cowling featured a "90S" badge and 70-mm BMW badge. The tank badges were initially enamel, but soon changed to plastic, and glued into place. BMW also added "900 cc" decals on the sidecovers, a helmet holder near the tire pump, and a tire pressure decal on the rear fender. Footpegs were round Denfeld, and the passenger footpegs were adjustable. U.S. versions were also fitted with three round reflectors at the rear, two on the license plate bracket and one on the fender.

A three-way-adjustable, double-acting hydraulic steering damper mounted under the steering head. The steering-damper knob turned a shaft inside the steering head tube, moving the damper away from the steering head axis 5/8 inch on the first setting, and 1-1/4 inch on the second setting. This provided a very effective damping adjustment.

The handbook for the R90S also covered /6 models, and the toolkit, BMW towel, tire patches, and tire pump, were like those of the /5 series, but without the exhaust-pipe and carburetor wrenches.

BMW offered a set of panniers and pannier frames as optional equipment on the R90S. Panniers were the same as those offered on the /5 and /6 series, but the R90S pannier frames differed in having a larger bolt-on rear brace to clear the rear-seat cowling. Large, high, and wide engine protection bars (from the /5) were also an option, but these detracted from the R90S's appearance.

ELECTRICS, CONTROLS, AND INSTRUMENTS

Switchgear and Horn

For the R90S and /6 series, BMW replaced the old plunger ignition switch with a combined ignition and light switch on the left headlight mounting bracket. The separate Neiman steering head lock remained, and as with the /5, the key for this lock operated the seat lock and also the optional fuel tank cap lock. BMW carried over onto the R90S and /6 series the /5's Hella handlebar switches, and gave the new models a new Bosch 0320 143 025 12-volt, 400-Hz horn, with a specific horn for the United States. From October 1973 the company fitted a special city horn for models sold in New York City. All horns were round, with a chrome-plated center section, similar to those of the first /5s.

Instruments and Warning Lights

One of the most noticeable developments on the /6 series, and the R90S in particular, was the new instrument layout. Not only was there a separate speedometer and tachometer, the R90S also received a clock and voltmeter mounted in the fairing. The new 85-mm MotoMeter instruments featured black faces with white numbers, and the 1974 instruments incorporated an aluminum ring inside the outer cover. The lenses were glare resistant, and for the first time on a BMW motorcycle the speedometer now incorporated a trip odometer. The speedometer read to 140 miles per hour, or 220 kilometers per hour, and the 8,500-rpm tachometer redlined at 7,000 rpm. The speedometer for the R90S with 1:3.00 final drive was a W=1.112 (miles per hour), or W=0.691 (kilometers per hour). Some early examples for the United States were inadvertently fitted with a W=1.144 speedometer designed for use with the 1.3.09 R90/6 final drive, resulting in optimistic speedometer and odometer readings.

Also new were the set of five warning lights between the two instruments. These were labeled in English for U.S. models: Brake Fail (red), Neutral (green), Gen (red), Oil (orange), and an

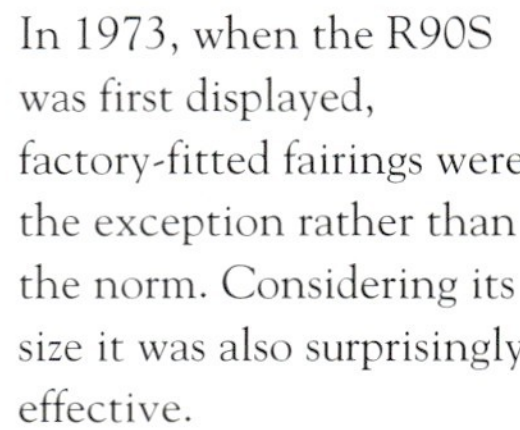

In 1973, when the R90S was first displayed, factory-fitted fairings were the exception rather than the norm. Considering its size it was also surprisingly effective.

The R90S seat had a fiberglass base and rear cowling with a specific "90S" emblem.

R90S Dimensions, Weights, and Performance

Overall width	29.1 inches
Saddle height	32.7 inches
Overall length	85.8 inches
Overall height	47.6 inches
Wheelbase	57.7 inches
Weight including oil but without fuel	452 pounds
Weight including oil and fuel	474 pounds
Top speed	Over 124 mph
Standing kilometer	25.3 seconds

Shared with the R90/6 were the sidecover decals.

indicator light (yellow) for the turn signals. European versions had German labels: Bremse, O, Batt., and Oel. The blue high-beam indicator was included in the tachometer, and the entire instrument panel was easily removed, as it incorporated a printed circuit board rather than individual wire connectors.

Headlamp, Taillight, and Turn-Signals

BMW gave the R90S and /6 series a larger 7.1-inch (180 mm) Bosch 0 303 550 002 60/55-watt H4 headlamp. The black headlight body was now plastic. The Hella taillight and aluminum-bodied, rectangular Hella TBB 26 turn signals were the same as the /5.

The turn signal bodies were changed from aluminum to black plastic from 1975.

1975 R90S

Apart from problems with the gearbox collapsing, the R90S was virtually trouble free from the outset, but there were a number of small developments for the 1975 model year. The engine unit was carried over unchanged for the start of the year, but after numbers 4080437 and 4980304 (United States), the company updated the engine with a new crankshaft, front main bearing, flywheel, and stronger (11x1.5-mm) flywheel retaining bolts. The ignition advance unit also received new springs.

The rear gearbox cover still provided for a kickstart, but this was now an option. To improve gear selection, BMW fitted new shifting forks for first and second gears, from numbers 4081390 and 4980730 (United States) and added the option of a five-speed close-ratio gearbox. A larger 26x7x16-mm oil seal prevented oil leaks from the gear shift lever. As most examples no longer featured a kickstart, BMW substituted a slightly more powerful Bosch Type 0 001 157 015 DF .6-horsepower starter motor. This increased the short-circuit starting current to 320 amps (from 290 amps).

From the start of the year's production, BMW fitted new fork legs, a new front hub, and a larger-diameter (17-mm) axle. From number 4081153 and U.S. number 4980520, BMW substituted new fork damping tubes and a stronger damping ring. These new dampers provided more compression damping and not only stiffened the suspension, but reduced the fork travel to 7.9 inches (200 mm). The 17-mm axle also contributed to more secure handling.

The 38-mm ATE black anodized front brake calipers were unchanged, as was the master cylinder, but there was a new front brake light switch. The twin 260-mm stainless-steel discs were drilled for 1975, with 200 holes designed to minimize fade in the dry, prevent the formation of water film in the wet, and reduced unsprung weight. They were cadmium-plated before being surface ground for improved cosmetics.

New black Magura dogleg-type levers graced the R90S from 1975 on. The brake lever included a new nipple for the cable attachment. Also new were the clutch-lever bracket and new integrated Hella handlebar switches (with the horn and light buttons on the left and engine start and turn signals rather idiosyncratically positioned on the right). A progressive-action twist-grip assembly had a faster-action 40-stroke cam bevel gear and chain more suitable for the longer stroke of the R90S's 38-mm Dell'Orto carburetors. The cam's

Although there were a few developments for 1975, the silver smoke R90S looked almost identical to the 1974 version. This U.S.-specification model (number 4 981 251) is unrestored, but has an aftermarket fork brace.

progressive action significantly improved throttle response. An accompanying new throttle cable and an additional cable adjuster incorporated at the top of the carburetor made it easier to synchronize the carburetors. This was always a problem with the Dell'Orto carburetors.

Colors for 1975 were named after racetracks, so silver smoke became TT Silver Smoke. A second color, Daytona Orange (code 510) was also offered for 1975. The pinstripes were now painted, and a suitable gold paint (code 104) was supplied for the TT Silver Smoke, or Fire Red (code 107) for the Daytona Orange. Two plastic knobs, rather than wing nuts, now retained the fuel tank.

While the general cockpit layout was unchanged, BMW began fitting a new MotoMeter speedometer and tachometer during 1975, after supplies of the earlier type were exhausted. These were still black-faced with white numerals, but with smaller graduation marks and no aluminum ring. Other changes for 1975 included an ignition switch with marked positions, a revised ignition key, a new wiring harness with new connectors for the headlight and parking light, and a new starter relay. The Hella turn

There were drilled front disc brakes for 1975, and a larger diameter axle. All U.S. models featured the fork-leg reflectors.

For 1975 there were new dogleg Magura clutch and brake levers.

Also new were the Hella handlebar switches, with the light and horn switches on the left.

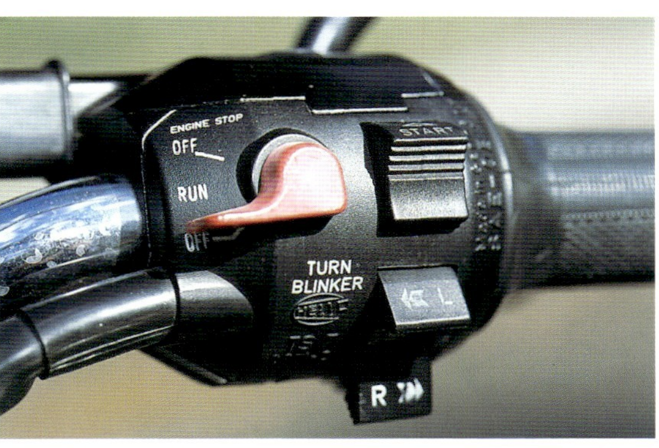

The start and turn signal switches were on the right. These switches were fitted from 1975 through 1976.

Although the warning lights were unchanged, the 1975 instruments had different faces. This is the U.S. speedometer.

signals now featured bodies of low-reflective black plastic rather than aluminum.

1976 R90S

Visually the 1976 R90S seemed identical to the 1975 model, but there were many improvements, particularly to the engine. With the development of the 980-cc /7 engine already well under way, most of the engine modifications made to the 1976 R90S were precursors to this uprated design, and shared with other /6s for 1976. As was usual with BMW production, some of these upgrades were introduced gradually as the parts supply for earlier versions was exhausted.

Engine and Drivetrain

The engine type was now known as the Type 247/76, and there were many developments. These included updated crankcases, cylinder heads, cylinders, pushrods, camshaft, and oil pump. The updated crankcases were designed to accept larger cylinder spigots and were reinforced around the front main bearing. There was also a deeper oil pan that moved the oil further from the crankshaft. Engine oil capacity of 2.25 liters was unchanged, but a longer oil dipstick was required for the deeper sump. The new crankshaft, front main bearing, and flywheel appeared during 1975, and after numbers 4090352 and U.S. 4990308, BMW began fitting an O-ring between the crankshaft and flywheel.

The cylinder heads were also new, with a longer 54-mm inlet valve guide, while retaining the 48-mm exhaust valve guide. There were new rocker arms (centered in the cylinder head with special fit rings), new rocker arm support blocks, and a spacer for the pushrod supports. The new 275-mm pushrods were a three-part hollow aluminum-and-steel construction similar to that used on the V-8 automobile engines and were 20 percent lighter. These pushrods expanded more consistently with the aluminum cylinders, and BMW could have specified tighter valve clearances, but didn't until 1977.

New cylinders included revised pushrod tubes. BMW used a base gasket to seal the new cylinders, and "Hylomar" sealing compound and O-rings to seal the cylinder studs.

Although the camshaft valve lift and timing were as before, the camshaft spindle diameter was increased from 12 to 20 mm, along with larger bushes and seals in the revised timing chain case. The larger-diameter spindle was intended to reduce camshaft flex, with a reduction in oil seal wear and improved valve operation. Inside, BMW updated the oil pump with a new inner rotor, tighter clearances between the oil pump rotor and pump housing, and a tighter gap between the inner and outer rotor. The Woodruff key locating the oil pump rotor on the camshaft was increased to 5.0x6.5 mm, although the sprocket key was as before. During 1976 a new engine breather cover was introduced.

Changes to the gearbox to improve shifting included a new gear shift cam plate and detent spring, and there was a new neutral-indicator switch. The transmission cases were also strengthened. The electrical and ignition system was largely unchanged, except for a new Bosch D 120 915 158 14V 20A diode carrier and slightly higher-rated Bosch G1 14V 17A 22/240 W alternator. The maximum output was 250 watts with 18 amps of current. The ignition points rubber strip was now 3.2 mm instead of 2.5 mm.

Chassis

BMW made a number of chassis improvements for 1976, including heavier gusseting on the swingarm directly in front of the rear tire, and a new-style chassis identification plate. The braking system was also updated, with larger-piston (40-mm) ATE black-anodized front brake calipers, new brake pads, and a new master cylinder with a larger (17.46-mm) piston. The larger pistons worked together to get more braking power for the same amount of hand pressure on the lever. The calipers were marked "40" to indicate their piston size. A coil clip replaced the hose clamp retaining the master cylinder to the frame, and a new Bowden brake cable connected the handlebar lever to the master cylinder. The fork sliders were also different, with 72.5-mm (up from 72.2-mm) mounts for the larger brake calipers. Tolerance between the fork tube and fork slider was reduced to .1 mm (instead of .24 mm). Other small changes included two milled nuts rather than wing nuts retaining the rear of the fuel tank to the frame, and a new clutch lever.

The 1975 R90S still presented an imposing image. Compare the slightly different handlebar shape of this U.S.-specification model with that of the earlier European-specification machine.

End of the Road

In 1976 the R90S cost $3,965 and was one of the most expensive motorcycles available. But it was well worth it. The R90S provided unparalleled performance and comfort, with the highest quality equipment. It was debatable whether the R90S could justify a price $600 higher than for the similar R90/6, but BMW went on to sell as many R90Ss as it could make. While the R90S isn't particularly rare, in the author's opinion it is the most desirable BMW motorcycle of the modern era. Later S versions may handle better and provide superior performance and ease of use, but it is no coincidence the R90S has garnered a cult following. R90S production also coincided with a period of particularly excellent quality from the Spandau plant. Of all the air-cooled twins, those built from

R90S Production

Model Year	Production Dates	1973	1974	1975	1976	Total
1974	09/1973-08/1974	986	4,067			5,053
1974 (United States)	09/1973-08/1974		1,005			1,005
1975	08/1974-08/1975		1,376	3,299		4,675
1975 (United States)	08/1974-08/1975		677	1,061		1,738
1976	09/1974-07/1976			912	2,812	3,724
1976 (United States)	09/1974-07/1976			584	676	1,260
						17,455

Daytona Orange was offered from 1975 and became the most popular color for 1976. Along with a deeper sump, inside the engine were a number of improvements. This is number 4092117, placing it toward the end of the production run.

The size of the ATE brake caliper pistons was increased for 1976, and the black caliper body was stamped with "40" to indicate 40 mm.

All R90Ss included a cockpit-mounted voltmeter and analog clock with white faces, flanked by tire and oil information.

1974 to 1976 seem to have been put together with more care and will cover higher mileages with fewer problems.

With its bold styling, stunning colors, and high-performance engine, the R90S was also the motorcycle that elevated BMW into the world of the Superbike. It was the R90S that formed the basis of the only successful BMW Superbike racers, and when Steve McLaughlin led Reg Pridmore home in the 1976 Daytona Superbike race, Daytona Orange took on a new meaning. Pridmore went on to win the 1976 AMA Superbike Championship, and the R90S became the classic BMW motorcycle of the 1970s.

Chapter 4

R90/6, R75/6, and R60/6

Along with the spectacular R90S, BMW released a replacement for the /5 series, known as the /6 series. The new series included three models: he largest was the 900-cc R90/6. Next was the 750-cc R75/6. Smallest was the 600-cc R60/6. As demand for the small R50/5 was low, and virtually nonexistent in the United States, the 500-cc model disappeared, and the R60/6 became the base model. The /6 continued where the /5 left off, but with a five-speed gearbox, front disc brake on the R90/6 and R75/6, and a revised instrument layout. The R90/6 proved especially successful in the United States, and by the end of its production in 1976 had established itself as the most popular BMW motorcycle up to that time, with nearly 10,000 sold.

1974 R90/6, R75/6, and R60/6

Essentially, the /6 models were very similar to the R90S, but there were a few specific differences for the touring models. Most of these were to the chassis and bodywork, while the engines of the R90/6 and R75/6 were remarkably similar to that of the R90S. The R60/6 was essentially an updated R60/5.

Engine and Drivetrain

As with the /5, uniformity of many engine components marked the /6 (and R90S). The engine designation, Type 247, was the same as for the

Replacing the R75/5, the R75/6 looked very similar but was updated and more modern in a number of areas. The R90/6 was virtually identical to this R75/6, and only decals and emblems distinguished the two. Opposite: The /6 engine was similar to that of the R90S, with a finned alternator cover. The cylinders weren't painted black. This 1976 example has a later-model (even larger) sump.

/6 Chassis Numbers

Type	Numbers	Model Year	Production Dates
R60/6	2910001 to 2920000	1974	09/73–08/74
R60/6	2920001 to 2930000	1975	09/74–08/75
R60/6	2960001 to 2970000	1976	09/75–08/76
R60/6 (United States)	4900001 to 4910000	1974	09/73–08/74
R60/6 (United States)	4920001 to 4925000	1975	09/74–08/75
R60/6 (United States)	4925001 to 4925914	1976	09/75–08/76
R75/6	4010001 to 4020000	1974	09/73–08/74
R75/6	4020001 to 4030000	1975	09/74–08/75
R75/6	4030001 to 4040000	1976	09/75–08/76
R75/6 (United States)	4910001 to 4920000	1974	09/73–08/74
R75/6 (United States)	4940001 to 4945000	1975	09/74–08/75
R75/6 (United States)	4945001 to 4947578	1976	09/75–08/76
R90/6	4040001 to 4050000	1974	09/73–08/74
R90/6	4050001 to 4060000	1975	09/74–08/75
R90/6	4060001 to 4070000	1976	09/75–08/76
R90/6 (United States)	4930001 to 4940000	1974	09/73–08/74
R90/6 (United States)	4960001 to 4970000	1975	09/74–08/75
R90/6 (United States)	4970001 to 4973316	1976	09/75–08/76

R90S. The new, stronger crankcases were shared with the R90S, and apart from the crankshaft for the R60/6, the entire lower end was also the same. The smaller R60/6 crankshaft could pass easily through the smaller aperture of the new crankcase. As the R75/6 crankshaft was identical to that of the R90/6 (and R90S), it was a relatively easy operation to convert an R75/6 to 898 cc. Considering the performance differential between the four new models, the similarity in engine specification was striking, and an example of clever model rationalization. The quoted weight of the three engines (with starter and carburetors but without ignition) was also similar. The R90/6 engine weighed the same 137.3 pounds (62.5 kilograms) as the R90S engine, while the R75/6 engine was the heaviest, at 143 pounds (64.9 kilograms). The R60/6 engine weighed 139.9 pounds (63.5 kilograms).

Along with the capacity, the cylinder heads of all three models varied. The R60/6 cylinder heads were identical to the R60/5's, and those of the R75/6 the same as the R75/5's. The R60/6 retained the 38- and 34-mm valves (98.5 and 97.5 mm long) and the R75/6 42- and 38-mm valves (98.8 mm long). The R90/6 valves were the same 42- and 40-mm as used on the R90S. This model rationalization extended to the camshafts, with still only two standard camshafts specified, the 284-degree camshaft for the R60/6, and the 308-degree camshaft for the two larger models (and the R90S). The valve guides on the R60/6, R75/5, and R90/6 were the longer 54 mm of the R75/5, rather than the shorter R90S type. The rockers on all /6 engines (as on the R90S engine) now pivoted in needle roller bearings, although on a touring engine this seemed unnecessary.

Pistons for the R60/6 and R75/6 were identical to those on the /5. The 90-mm pistons of the R90/6 were like those of the R90S but had a flatter dome for a lower 9.0:1 compression ratio. The check valve for the engine breather of the R90/6 was in the same position as that of the R90S, and lower than that for R60/6 and R75/6. The front alternator cover featured external ribbing and alternator cooling vents, but was slightly different than that of the R90S. The cylinders on /6s were plain aluminum, rather than painted black as on the R90S.

/6 Engine Specifications

Model	Bore (mm)	Stroke (mm)	Capacity (cc)	Compression Ratio	Horsepower DIN/SAE
R60/6	73.5	70.6	599	9.2:1	40@6400 rpm 46@6600 rpm
R75/6	82	70.6	745	9.0:1	50@6200 rpm 57/6400 rpm
R90/6	90	70.6	898	9.0:1	60@6500 rpm 67@6700 rpm

R90/6, R75/6, and R60/6 Carburetors

	R60/6	R75/6	R90/6
Left Carburetor	Bing 1/26/111	Bing 64/32/9	Bing 64/32/11
Right Carburetor	Bing 1/26/112	Bing 64/32/10	Bing 64/32/12
Main Jet	140	135	135
Needle Jet	2.68	2.70	2.68
Jet Needle No.	4	46-241	46-241
Needle Position	3	3	1
Idle Jet	35	45 44-950	45 44-950

Unlike the R90S, which featured a new air filter housing suitable for the larger carburetor intakes, the /6 aluminum housing was shared with the /5 series. The R60/6 retained the Bing 26-mm concentric-slide carburetors, initially without a choke, but from numbers 2911377 and U.S. 4900616, a choke was incorporated, with the usual Magura choke lever attached to the air filter housing. The same 32-mm Bing CV carburetors fitted to the R75/5 were also used on the R75/6 and R90/6. The R90/6 and R75/6 intake manifolds were the same 36-mm-diameter, 25-mm-long units used on the 1973 R75/5. The R60/6 retained the 26-mm-diameter manifolds. The /6 exhaust system was the same as that of the R90S, but the R90/6 was also offered with a specific U.S. muffler on motorcycles for California, Florida, and Oregon.

The Bosch G1 14V 20A 21/280 W alternator on the /6 series was more powerful than that on the R90S, and was rated at 280 watts and 20 amps. There was also a different Bosch regulator. The ignition advance unit for the R60/6 and R75/6 was the same as for the /5 versions, but the R90/6 unit was shared with the R90S. The spark plugs for the R90/6, and R75/6 were Bosch W200 T30, Beru 200/14/3A, or Champion N7Y. For the R60/6 the spark plugs were Bosch W230 T30, Beru 230/14/3A, or Champion N7Y.

The clutch and gearbox were also similar to that of the R90S, with the R90/6 receiving the heavier 2.8-mm clutch diaphragm spring. Both the R75/6 and R60/6 used the 2.6-mm R75/5 clutch spring, with the 2.4-mm R60/5 spring no longer specified. As with the /5, each model of the /6 had a different final drive ratio.

Chassis

Model rationalization continued with the chassis. The black-painted frame, rear subframe, and swingarm were the same as those of the R90S. All models shared the new 200-mm Simplex rear brake, rear suspension, and rear wheel with the R90S, but the front brake and fork legs were different. Although some early publicity photos showed /6s with rear shock absorbers without aluminum spring covers, production shock absorbers had these covers.

Like the R75/5, the R75/6 had black model-designation emblems on the crankcases.

/6 Final Drive Ratios

Model	Number of Teeth	Ratio
R60/6	11:37	1:3.36
R75/6	10:32	1:3.2
R90/6	11:34	1:3.09

While the R60/6 Duplex front brake was similar to the previous /5 unit, it featured a new ribbed casting and no longer came with a chrome cover. As with the rear brake, there were inspection holes to determine brake lining wear. Both the R75/6 and R90/6 front fork provided for a single front disc brake only, with one ATE brake caliper (with 38-mm piston) on the left. The ATE master cylinder piston for the single front disc was 14.29 mm, smaller than that of the R90S. A supplementary second disc brake was an expensive option, as it included a new fork leg, master cylinder, and brake caliper.

Although the front fork internals were also the same as those of the R90S, the /6 fork included a /5 steel upper triple clamp. The new lower fork triple clamp was as for the R90S, and the R60/6 fork legs were new, and specific for that model. The fork springs were also initially shorter than those of the R90S, at 21.18 inches (538 mm). After R60/6 number 2910998, R75/6 number 4012043, and R90/6 number 404461, the fork springs were changed to the longer R90S type. All /6s featured new headlight support brackets, and the 13-rib rubber fork gaiters of the /5.

There was a new tubular steel handlebar for the /6, a standard 23.4-inch (600-mm), and a broader 26.5-inch (680-mm) for the United States. The handlebars were fastened to the top triple clamp with polished aluminum clamps, and the twin round mirrors were chrome-plated, rather than

As with the R90S, the /6 rear drum brake was without the chrome-plated cover, and included brake lining inspection holes.

The Boge shock absorbers were also shared with the R90S.

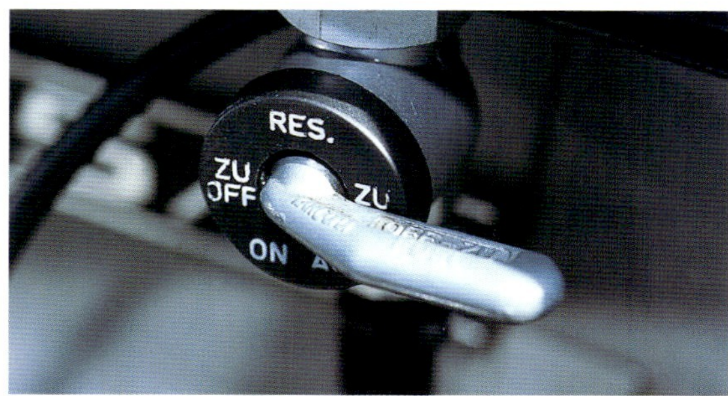

Most /6s came with these Karcoma fuel petcocks.

black as with the R90S. The aluminum Magura handlebar levers were anodized black.

The standard fuel tank for the /6 was 4.3 gallons (18 liters), with a larger 5.8 gallon (22-liter) tank optional, as it was with the 1973 /5s. The larger tank came with rubber kneepads, while these were no longer a feature on the smaller tank. Both featured glued plastic BMW badges. An even larger, 22-liter police specification fuel tank with lockable built-in toolbox was also optional. A wide range of colors were available, including black, white, metallic blue, metallic green, red, metallic curry, and metallic polaris. The hand-painted pinstripes were either black or white, fully encircling the side of the smaller tank. All the tank fittings, including fuel cap and petcocks were as for the R90S, with early Everbest petcocks replaced by Karcoma or Germa during 1974.

The dual Denfeld seat was similar to that of the 1973 /5, with longitudinal pleats on the upholstery, a white plastic bead, and a single chrome-plated grab bar at the rear. The seat also had a black model emblem on the tail. A shorter solo short seat was also an option through the 1976 model year.

The /6 fiberglass front fender wasn't shaped as deeply as that of the R90S, but a deeper police fender was offered as an option. This fender wasn't very practical, however, as it required removal to access the front wheel. In addition to the pressed steel brace between the fork legs, /6s also included a chrome-plated tubular stay that connected the rear of the fender to the lower fork leg. The fiberglass sidecovers were identical to those of the R90S, painted to match the tank and fenders. Some early brochures showed sidecovers without decals, but production models came with a decal indicating the capacity, "900 cc," "750 cc," or "600 cc."

The /6 instrument layout, with separate speedometer and tachometer with five warning lights, was shared with the R90S, but each speedometer was geared for a specific final drive. The R60/6 speedometer was W=1.244 (miles per hour) or W=.773 (kilometers per hour). For the

R90/6, R75/6, and R60/6 Dimensions, Weights and Performance

Overall width	29.1 inches
Saddle height	31.9 inches
Overall length	85.8 inches
Overall height	42.5 inches
Wheelbase	57.7 inches
Weight including oil but without fuel	441 pounds
Weight including oil and fuel	463 pounds

Type	R60/6	R75/6	R90/6
Top speed	104 mph	110 mph	117 mph
Standing kilometer	29.7 seconds	28.1 seconds	26.1 seconds

/6 Production 1974 Model Year

Model	Dates	1973	1974	Total
R60/6	09/73-08/74	448	1,229	1,677
R60/6 (United States)	01/74-08/74		827	827
R75/6	09/73-08/74	1,203	1,628	2,831
R75/6 (United States)	06/74-08/74		1,097	1,097
R90/6	09/73-08/74	3,049	1,922	4,971
R90/6 (United States)	01/74-08/74		2,218	2,218
				13,621

/6 Production 1975 Model Year

Model	Dates	1974	1975	Total
R60/6	08/74-08/75	1,575	2,293	3,868
R60/6 (United States)	08/74-07/75	593	510	1,103
R75/6	08/74-08/75	1,198	2,490	3,688
R75/6 (United States)	08/74-08/75	962	1,125	2,087
R90/6	08/74-08/75	984	2,327	3,311
R90/6 (United States)	08/74-08/75	1,802	2,461	4,263
				18,320

R75/6 there was a W=1.186 (miles per hour), or W=.737 (kilometers per hour), and the R90/6 had a W=1.112 (miles per hour) or W=.691 (kilometers per hour). As with the R90S, it was important for speedometer accuracy that the correct instrument be matched to the final drive ratio. Also shared with the R90S was the /5-style Hella handlebar switches, and cam-and-chain throttle assembly. As this was designed for smaller-bodied carburetors, it worked more satisfactorily on the /6 than it did on the R90S.

Options included the R90S fairing with voltmeter and clock, or a touring fairing with high windshield. The voltmeter and clock were also available as accessory pods mounted on top of the fork, and there were the usual options of a lockable fuel filler cap, engine protection bars, soft and hard luggage, and additional driving lights.

1975 R90/6, R75/6, and R60/6

Updates for 1975 mirrored those of the R90S. From R60/6 number 2921610 (U.S. number 4920662), R75/6 number 4020452 (U.S. 4940406), and R90/6 number 4050186 (U.S. 4980304), there was a new crankshaft. Toward the end of the 1975 model year (from R90/6 number 4050991 and U.S. number 4961904), there were new gearbox shifting forks. The suppressed voltage regulator now incorporated a vibration absorber, and was now the same as that on the R90S. As the kickstart was no longer standard, all /6s also received the more powerful starter motor. There were also new mixture chambers for the Bing CV carburetors this year.

For 1975 there were new fork legs to accommodate the larger, 17-mm axle. A drilled front brake disc was fitted to the R90/6 and R75/6. The R60/6 now had a new front brake plate. None of the /6 models received the new fork dampers of the R90S.

Following the success of Helmut Dahne and Hans Otto Butenuth in production racing and production-based racing in Europe, the colors for 1975 were named after racetracks. They included Monza Blue, Nürburg Green, Bol d'Or Red, Imola Silver, and Avus Black. Apart from the Imola Silver, with black pinstripes, all other colors were pinstriped with white. Metallic paint was available as an option.

Seat upholstery was changed for 1975 with cross pleats and no white bead. A BMW roundel replaced a specific model emblem on the tail, so seats were interchangeable between models.

All the /6s were fitted with the new ignition, handlebar switchgear, MotoMeter instruments, and twist-grip throttle as the R90S, but the /6 throttle came with a 33 cam rather than the 40 cam of the R90S. This year the /6 was offered with an optional touring package that included

One of the few distinguishing features between the R75/6 and R90/6 were the sidecover decals.

The seat, with a single passenger grab handle, was similar to that of the /5, as were the rubber gaiters on the forks. This 1976 R75/6 (number 4033222) has nonstandard shock absorbers and a 1978 gearshift setup. Missing on the rear of the seat is the round BMW emblem that was fitted to 1975

a windshield and the larger fuel tank, or a touring luxury package. With this came a full range of accessories.

1976 R90/6, R75/6, and R60/6

Although the 1976 /6s were visually identical to those of 1975, underneath were the myriad updates that also characterized the R90S that year. The new, stronger engine housing of the R90S was shared with the R90/6 and R75/6, while R60/6 featured a new engine housing specific to that model. All versions now had the deeper sump oil pan and new cylinders sealed with Hylomar compound. Only the low-compression version of the R60/6, suitable for poor fuel, now had the base gaskets. While the cylinder head specifications were unchanged, inside the cylinder heads were new rockers, and R90S valve guides (54-mm inlet and 48-mm exhaust). The 75/6 engine-breather check valve was moved to the same position as that of the R90/6, and all models were fitted with the same front alternator cover as the R90S. The R60/6 and R75/6 also received the R90/6 automatic ignition-advance unit.

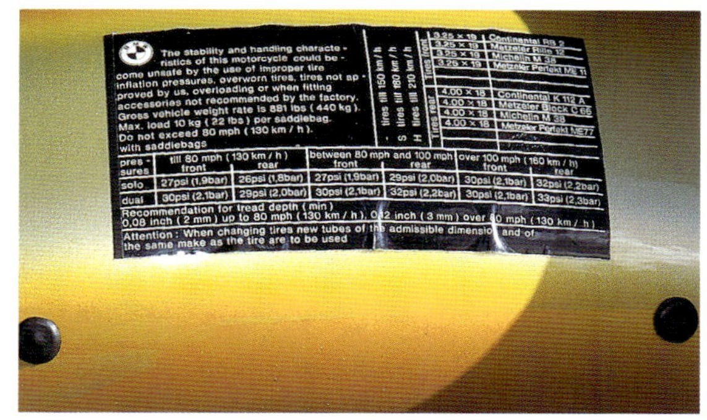

BMW /6 motorcycles featured several warning decals like this under the seat, on the rear fender.

From R60/6 number 2960660 (U.S. number 4925289), R75/6 number 4030398 (U.S. number 4945230), and R90/6 number 4060267 (U.S. number 4970610), an O-ring was installed between the crankshaft and flywheel. In the gearbox were the new cam plate and detent spring. The U.S. R60/6s and R75/6s received a lower final drive to improve top gear acceleration.

Revised speedometers accompanied the new final drive of the R60/6 and R75/6. The drive for the R60/6 was W=1.318 (miles per hour) or W=.819 (kilometers per hour). For the R75/6 the drive was W=1.244 (miles per hour) and W=.773

/6 Final Drive Ratios (U.S. models 1976)

	Number of Teeth	Ratio
R60/6	9:32	1:3.56
R75/6	11:37	1:3.36

(kilometers per hour). The R75/6 and R90/6 now featured a 40-mm brake caliper, along with a new master cylinder. Unlike on the R90S, the master cylinder wasn't correspondingly larger, the piston size remaining at 14.29 mm.

End of the Road

Although overshadowed by the more spectacular R90S, the /6 series were excellent motorcycles, and justifiably popular. They were well built and extremely reliable, and the R90/6 and R75/6 provided outstanding touring performance for the day. Although the R60/6 was underpowered, the R90/6 and the R75/6 epitomized the finest aspects of the boxer twin—quality, aesthetics, smoothness, and performance.

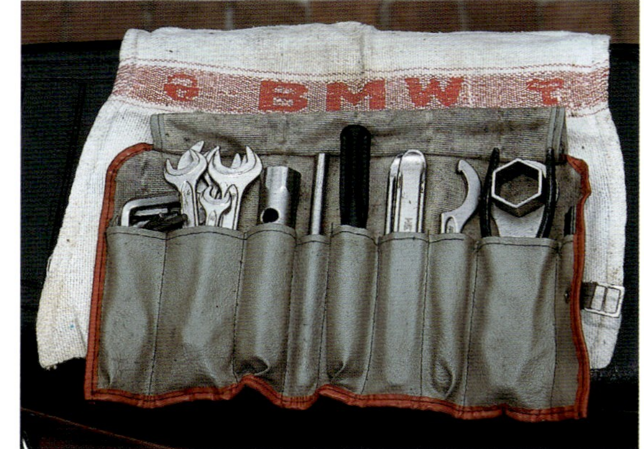

This R75/6 has a number of factory options, including the larger fuel tank, additional front disc brake, voltmeter, and clock. The /6 is one of the most handsome, and underrated, BMW motorcycles.
Left: Another distinguishing feature was the superb toolkit and embroidered towel.

/6 Production 1976 Model Year

Model	Dates	1975	1976	Total
R60/6	09/75-07/76		2,012	2,012
R60/6 (United States)	09/75-07/76		643	643
R75/6	09/75-07/76	1,955	3,351	5,306
R75/6 (United States)	09/75-07/76	1,166	1,412	2,578
R90/6	09/75-07/76	716	2,302	3,018
R90/6 (United States)	09/75-07/76	2,012	1,304	3,316
				16,873

Chapter 5

R100RS (1977–84)

Another classic modern BMW motorcycle is the 1977 R100RS, in many ways the most handsome of the entire genre.

Although the R90S changed the perception of BMW motorcycles as staid and boring machines, it still wasn't perfect. The R90S was both a styling triumph and a high-performance motorcycle, and while the handling was acceptable, there was some criticism of high-speed instability. This was probably due to a combination of frame flex and the high steering inertia caused by the handlebar-mounted fairing, so the next development of the top-of-the-line BMW touring motorcycle centered on a more aerodynamic and integrated frame-mounted fairing. The result was the R100RS, the initials representing Rennsport, or Racing Sport, and harking back to the bevel-drive, double-overhead-camshaft racers of 1954. When it was released in August 1976, the R100RS didn't really bear any relationship to those magnificent racers, but it caused a sensation similar to that of the R90S three years earlier. And with it, BMW created another classic motorcycle, just as distinctive as the R90S, and functionally superior. Today, aerodynamically integrated full fairings are de rigueur for motorcycles, and the R100RS was the pioneer.

1977 R100RS

Following his success with the R90S, Hans Muth was asked to style a motorcycle emphasizing rider protection and aerodynamic function. Again he was successful, and the R100RS was the first production motorcycle to offer a fully integrated fairing that not only provided outstanding weather protection, it also contributed to the stability of the motorcycle. Even nearly 30 years on, the R100RS fairing remains a benchmark in motorcycle fairing design efficiency. Because of the larger frontal area, top speed was less than that of the R90S, but the high-speed handling was superior, as was rider comfort. In the author's experience, there is still no fairing that can match that of an R100RS for ultimate weather protection in a sport-touring motorcycle. Even the later K100RS fairing wasn't as effective as that of the R100RS. Although the R90S continued as the R100S, this model was relegated down the lineup as the R100RS established itself as the range leader. True to form, it also set a new price benchmark, selling for a staggering $4,595 in 1977. A few prototypes were built from March 1976, but regular production commenced in August 1976, for the 1977 model year.

Engine and Drivetrain

Many of the engine updates for the R100RS, and its /7 series stablemates, were introduced on the R90S and /6 for the 1976 model year. Yet while the R100RS engine carried the same Type 247/76 internal engine designation, the new engine was known as Type M65*. There were only a few developments from the final 1976 900-cc engines. The deeper oil pan introduced during 1976 was a feature of all /7s, but only an option for the R100RS for California, Florida, and Oregon until 1979 (number 6 183 254). In usual BMW fashion, there was continual evolution of the engine design, with annual development. Although the silumin crankcases were further reinforced to withstand the higher horsepower, the weight of the engine was identical to the earlier R90S at 62.5 kilograms (137.7 pounds).

R100RS Carburetors (1977–80)

Left Carburetor	Bing 94/40/105
Right Carburetor	Bing 94/40/106
Main Jet	170
Needle Jet	2.68
Jet Needle No.	46-341
Needle Position	2
Idle Jet	45

R100RS Engine Specifications

Bore (mm)	Stroke (mm)	Capacity (cc)	Compression Ratio	Horsepower DIN
94	70.6	980	9.5:1	70@7250 rpm

R100RS Chassis Numbers (1977–84)

Type	Numbers	Model Year	Production Dates
R100RS	6080001 to 6080013	1976	03/76–05/76
R100RS	6080014 to 6085159	1977	08/76–06/77
R100RS	6086001 to 6095000	1978	09/77–08/78
R100RS	6095001 to 6100000	1979	09/78–08/80
R100RS	6223001 to 6224000	1979–80	09/78–08/80
R100RS	6075001 to 6080000	1981	09/80–08/81
R100RS	6390001 to 6397000	1981—84	09/80–10/84
R100RS	6180001 to 6180059	1976	05/76–08/76
R100RS (United States)	6180114 to 6181263	1977	10/76–08/77
R100RS (United States)	6182501 to 6183592	1978	09/77–08/78
R100RS (United States)	6185001 to 6186000	1979–80	09/78–08/80
R100RS (United States)	6225001 to 6229000	1981—84	09/80–10/84
R100RS (United States)	6308001 to 6308100		

The large frontal area of the RS fairing limited top-end performance, but contributed to excellent rider protection and improved stability over the R90S.

Early silver R100RSs (1977 and 1978) also had specific model-designation engine emblems highlighted in blue.

The most noticeable update to the R100RS engine was the increase in displacement, through 94-mm pistons and cylinders. Constructed of a new lightweight aluminum alloy by either Mahle or Kolben Schmidt, the pistons weighed the same as the previous 90-mm type. The cylinders had thicker and shorter cooling fins to reduce noise, and were no longer painted black (as on the R90S). The piston clearances were also tighter (on all /7s), with the maximum wear limit of 0.0031-inch (0.08 mm) rather than 0.0046 inch (0.12 mm).

To cope with the increased crankcase pressure generated by the larger cylinders, BMW improved the crankcase ventilation system. Along with a small baffle chamber cast into the crankcase starter cavity, there was a new breather housing that included a small rectangular top hat and new outlet, a longer (13-inch) hose, and a new intake bell. The system still ventilated into the right carburetor intake.

Inside the cylinder head were larger inlet valves, now 44 mm (98.8 mm long). Both inlet and exhaust valve guides were 48 mm. There was no change to the previous 308-degree camshaft, or the camshaft drive system, but longer (8x45-mm, and 8x55-mm) studs retained the camshaft drive housing. Although BMW gave the R100RS engine the lighter aluminum pushrods of the 1976 R90S, it wasn't until 1977 that tighter valve clearances of 0.004 inch (0.10 mm) for the inlet and 0.006 inch (0.15 mm) for the exhaust were specified to reduce noise.

Changes to the lubrication system included a gasket for the oil pump pickup in the sump and a new outer cover plate for the oil filter. The oil filter included a steel shim and O-ring, and it was important to fit the shim into the crankcase first.

One of the most obvious changes was the new angular rocker covers, now black anodized with polished fins. These were a little larger and heavier than the older round rocker covers that first appeared on the R68 of 1952. The result was a slightly wider engine than before, and as there were different covers for left and right, "L" and "R" marks were cast inside the covers. Special R100RS engine emblems, black with sliver and blue highlighting, completed the cosmetic alterations.

Rather than the concentric Dell'Orto carburetors of the R90S, the R100RS received Bing 40-mm Type 94 CV carburetors. With these carburetors came 40-mm intake manifolds, a new airbox, and a revised intake bell on top of the air filter box. Larger, 40x1.5-mm exhaust header pipes also helped make the R100RS the most powerful boxer to date. Also new were the star exhaust-pipe nuts and an 87-mm muffler. The larger exhausts came with 42-mm clamps, but the smaller 38-mm exhaust header pipes

All 1977 R100RSs retained the earlier gearshift setup. The kickstart was an option.

R100RS Competition Gearbox Ratios

1st Gear	3.38:1
2nd Gear	2.43:1
3rd Gear	1.93:1
4th Gear	1.67:1
5th Gear	1.50:1

(with 40-mm clamps) were listed as an option for 1977. All California, Oregon, and Florida R100RSs (through number 6183254) had the smaller header pipes and a more restrictive muffler.

The clutch was a 180-mm single-disc unit, similar to that of the R90S, also using the 2.8-mm diaphragm spring, but with a heavier-duty antiwarp clutch disc. The flywheel was new, slightly thinner, and lighter, weighing 7 pounds, 12 ounces. This was to maintain the same 15-pound, 12-ounce weight of the whole clutch-and-flywheel assembly with the new heavier clutch disc. The number of teeth on the flywheel was increased to 94. Although the transmission case received lengthwise exterior ribbing, the five-speed gearbox internals were unchanged. There was a different new neutral light switch. An alternative close-ratio sporting or competition transmission was also available. The kick-start mechanism remained an option.

The standard final drive ratio for the European R100RS was 1:3.00 (33:11), with a higher 1:2.91 (32:11) for the United States. Some early U.S. R100RSs came with the European final drive.

New for the R100RS, and all /7s, were the angular rocker covers and larger insulated spark plug caps.

Electrical System and Ignition

The R100RS retained the smaller alternator of the R90S, the 250-watt Bosch G1 14V 18A 22/240W. BMW also fitted a 0.6-horsepower Bosch starter motor that was identical to that of the R90S, but the starter transmission ratio was increased to aid starting in colder temperatures, and a Bosch relay was added to the starter circuit. The Varta battery was now a 28-Ah. The ignition system featured the same Bosch coils and contact breaker (with 31 degrees of advance) but with new spark plug leads and caps, and Bosch W225 T30, Beru 230/14/3A, or Champion N6Y spark plugs.

Frame and Suspension

In creating the frame and swingarm used on the R100RS and /7 series, BMW started with the 1976 /6 frame and added a second transverse tube between the front double downtubes, added gusseting around the steering head, and built it of thicker tubing. This frame was designated Type 247/77.

BMW made substantial updates in modifying the old /6 fork for use on the R100RS. First, it modified the dampers (one less bleed hole and less oil capacity) and springs (shorter than on the other /7s, at 21.38 inches or 543 mm) for a softer ride in the middle range of fork movement and stiffer at the end. Then it reduced the steering angle to 35 degrees (from 42 degrees) for use with the fairing. The trail was increased to 95 mm (3.74 inches), while the rake was 28 degrees. As part of the R100RS's accentuated black image, the fork legs were painted black, and fork legs for the U.S. market were fitted with rectangular

Also specific to 1977 and silver 1978 model R100RSs were blue-anodized ATE 40-mm brake calipers, and the fork legs were black.

Although cast wheels were listed as an option, most 1977 R100RSs had wire-spoked wheels with aluminum rims. The rims were highlighted with two blue lines on each side.

The Boge shock absorbers had fully exposed black springs, without the aluminum top cover.

reflectors. The rear Boge shock absorbers were as on the /6 series, with three-way adjustable black springs, but were now without top polished alloy spring covers.

Wheels, Tires, and Brakes

Most 1977 R100RSs were fitted with spoked wheels with the usual aluminum rims, cast hubs, and 40 straight-pull stainless-steel spokes. These wheels were the same size as those of the previous /6—1.85Bx19-inch on the front and 2.15Bx18-inch on the rear—but two blue pinstripes on each wheel rim distinguished the R100RS wheels. Cast-alloy "snowflake" pattern wheels were listed as a $400 option for the R100RS only, the rear a 2.50x18-inch. While these cast wheels were featured on R100RSs in brochures and many early road tests, they weren't generally available during 1977 due to supply problems. If the chassis numbers for early bikes produced in March 1976 are any guide, they were possibly fitted to only three 1976 European prototypes and four U.S. prototypes. These alloy wheels were designed by BMW but were initially built by FPS in Italy, and were a considerable 6 pounds heavier than the spoked type. Although undoubtedly more rigid, they were also prone to cracking, and all wheels manufactured prior to the end of 1982 were recalled during 1984. The replacement wheels looked similar but included additional support around the spokes. Tires were Continental Twins (matched front and rear) or Metzeler Block C66 Touring, in 3.25-H19 and 4.00-H18 as original equipment. The Continentals offered better grip and handling.

The perforated dual front disc brakes were now quoted at 10.39 inches (264 mm) in the official manual. Calipers were 40-mm ATEs of the single-piston floating types, and they were anodized blue. The ATE 17.46-mm master cylinder still resided underneath the fuel tank, and the brake lines were a similar rubber/steel combination, but spaced to clear the fairing. The rod-operated 200-mm rear drum brake was as before on spoked-wheel models. Rear brakes on the few cast-wheel versions incorporated air scoops for cooling, with protective plastic screens over the scoops.

Handlebars, Levers, and Mirrors

A much narrower, almost clip-on style, handlebar distinguished the R100RS from other sporting BMWs. Short enough to fit completely inside the fairing, the 21.6x0.87-inch (548x22-mm) flat handlebar provided a very aggressive riding position that placed more weight on the rider's wrists. This undoubtedly contributed to the R100RS's improved stability over the R90S, but made the R100RS more suitable for high-speed, rather than low-speed, touring duties. The handlebar levers were black Magura dogleg type, with the same

Magura handgrips as on the /6 series. The new rectangular rearview mirrors were also black.

Fairing, Fuel Tank, Side Panels, and Fenders

By far the most innovative feature of the R100RS was the injection-molded fiberglass fairing. Wind tunnel designed, the beautifully finished 20.9-pound (9.5-kilogram) fairing was claimed to reduce air resistance by 5.4 percent, front wheel lift by 17.4 percent, and side yawing by 60 percent over the R90S. It was built in seven sections, plus a low windshield. The front upper section included a rubber headlight shell and a Sekurit safety glass cover that incorporated five orange lines. These were purely a styling addition with no functional value and did seem a strange inclusion. The design of the windshield, with its small kick-up and decorative beading also came in for some criticism, as it generated some turbulence around the rider's helmet.

The front fairing section was a grill that allowed air to the front of the engine, and the lower sections could be removed for riding in hot weather. These lowers were a one-piece design on 1977 models, requiring the exhaust pipes to be removed before the lowers could be removed. Two black-painted tubular steel brackets, incorporated into the bracket welded to the head stock, rigidly located the top of the fairing and served as mounts for the mirrors. Two additional tubes bolted to the sides, with a third set of pressed-steel brackets below the cylinders. The lateral fairing bracket passing underneath the fuel tank was very close to the main battery cable and could chafe through the cable, causing an electrical short and possibly a fire. Sealing the fairing from underneath were two rubber cups encircling the fork tubes, these also restricted maneuverability at low speeds. Open-cell foam filled the space between the fairing and the front frame downtubes.

BMW offered only one color on 1977 R100RSs: flat metallic silver top coated with clear lacquer and pinstriped in blue. The pinstriping generally wasn't as carefully applied as in the past. Standard on all /7s, including the R100RS, was the stylish 6.3-gallon (24-liter) steel fuel tank of the R90S, updated with a new black flush-mounted lockable filler cap, with a separate key to the ignition. The design of the tank cap wasn't perfect on early examples and could sometimes rotate without unlocking. The tank was retained at the rear by two plastic threaded knobs. Not only was the tank constructed in two halves as before, it incorporated an internal expansion chamber to reduce fuel overflow.

The body side panels were flat black, with blue "1,000 cc" decals. Fenders were similar to those of

The cockpit of the R100RS was similar to that of the R90S, but the handlebar was even narrower and lower. The handlebar switches were slightly different, with thumb extensions on the lower controls, and the handlebar featured an automotive-style pad. Also setting the R100RS apart was the improved ignition switch location.

All 1977 and 1978 R100RSs included this vented section of the fairing in front of the engine.

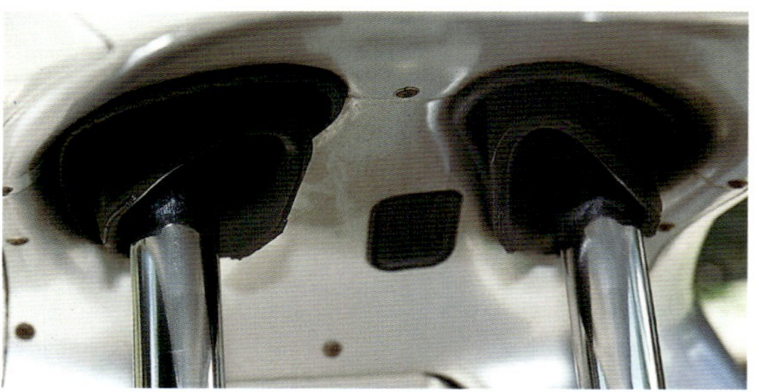

Sealing the fairing underneath around the fork tubes were rubber cups, although many owners removed these to reduce steering restriction.

New for 1977 was a lockable flush-mounted fuel cap. This was prone to turning without unlocking.

This European-specification 1977 R100RS (number 6080917) has withstood the ravishes of time amazingly well. Apart from the fairing headlight Duro-glas, it is very original. Flat metallic silver was the only color available in the first year.

The five orange lines in the headlight safety glass were purely a cosmetic feature, with no practical function.

the R90S. The front fender was also painted silver with blue pinstriping and included a steel brace linking the fork legs. The rear fender was flat black.

Seat, Badges, and Frame Fittings

Two seats were offered for the R100RS, a solo (almost one and a half) sport seat and the R90S-type dual seat. Both seats included a BMW roundel on their tail and were lockable. The dual seat included a black grab rail. BMW also fitted the RS with two helmet locks and the usual lift-out plastic tool tray under the seat, along with a useful rear storage compartment that was quite large on the solo-seat version.

Locks for 1977 included separate keys for the ignition and fuel filler cap. New rectangular Denfeld footpeg rubbers were fitted for 1977. Passenger footpegs were omitted on solo-seat RSs. The R100RS was the only model to retain the three-position, two-stage steering damper as standard equipment this year. As in the past, the 26-piece toolkit was extremely comprehensive, and included a wrench for adjusting the steering head bearings and swingarm. Also included were a tire repair kit and a tire pump under the seat. European models also included a first-aid kit that fitted under the seat padding, but this compromised seat comfort.

Switchgear and Horns

Although the layout of the Hella handlebar switches was the same as before, the right indicator switch now included an extension wing for ease of operation with the thumb, as did the left high/low beam and flasher switch. Twin Fiamm horns, a 410 Hz on the right and 510 Hz on the left, were louder than before. Unfortunately, these horns were mounted below the fuel tank, so the sound bounced off the inner fairing panels and could be disconcerting for the rider.

Instruments and Warning Lights

Although the R100RS's instrument layout closely followed that of the R90S, the instruments and warning lights were even more integrated into the fairing. The speedometer and tachometer were still black with white numerals, and mounted on the top triple clamp. An automotive-style plastic cover concealed the handlebar. The ignition key was more conveniently located between the voltmeter and electric clock, and the speedometer was specific for the fitted final drive ratio. On U.S. examples with the 2.91 final drive, the mile-per hour speedometer was a W=1.078. The speedometer for a 3.00 final drive was W=1.112.

Headlamp, Taillight, and Turn Indicators

There was no change to the excellent 7-inch (180-mm) Bosch H4 headlight, and the Hella taillight

R100RS Dimensions, Weights, and Performance (1977–80)

Overall width	29.37 inches
Saddle height	32.3 inches
Overall length	85.8 inches
Overall height	51.6 inches
Wheelbase	57.7 inches
Weight including oil but without fuel	463 pounds
Weight including oil and fuel	507 pounds
Top speed	Over 124 mph
0–100 mph	12.6 seconds

R100RS Production 1977 Model

Model	Dates	1976	1977	Total
R100RS	08/76-07/77	1,418	3,741	5,159
R100RS (United States)	08/76-06/77	542	721	1,263
				6,422

A sporting solo seat was an option for 1977, and remained so until 1984.

Also new for 1977 were rectangular Denfeld footpeg rubbers.

in polished black surround was also as before. There were the usual round reflectors at the rear on U.S. models, and the rear Hella turn-signals in black housings. The front turn signals were flush mounted in the fairing, as was a horizontal rectangular parking light above the headlight.

1978 R100RS

There were only detail changes to the R100RS for the 1978 model year, and the price rose dramatically, to $5,295 in the United States. And if you lived on the West Coast you had to pay an additional $100 for the RS experience. As the most expensive production motorcycle available in the United States, the R100RS was now elevated beyond mainstream motorcycling into the world of luxury appendages. Of course, the higher price didn't detract from its functional excellence, but it did mean that the numbers sold in the United States were relatively small. In other parts of the world the R100RS, while still expensive, didn't command such a premium.

Engine updates were few for 1978. Piston wrist pins were now retained by a Seeger-pattern circlip. The Bing 40-mm carburetors had a new float needle. Starting with number 6 183 255, BMW began fitting U.S models with a double-sided breather venting into both carburetor intakes and a new crankcase top cover. The new cover replaced the previous single-sided type, and featured "BMW" lettering cast in each side, an integral air intake, and a T-junction with three breather hoses (a 9.5-inch hose connected to two shorter hoses). At the same time, the U.S. R100RS received the deeper sump, new cylinder heads, new mufflers, and slightly leaner carburetor jetting (160 main jets).

All 1978 versions featured a new camshaft, with the same duration and valve lift, but advanced 6 degrees. With the new camshaft came a new camshaft drive sprocket (without a tachometer-drive spiral gear), and a new timing-chain case. The angular black rocker covers now had "L" and "R" cast into the external top surfaces to make identification easier.

In an effort to further improve gear shifting, BMW modified the gear lever so it pivoted on the rider's footpeg attachment and attached to the small shifting lever with a U rod that was covered with a rubber bellows. Showing typical thoroughness to practicality, BMW added a grease nipple to the pivot.

BMW made only minor changes to the fork for 1978. Filler covers were now black instead of chrome and were fitted without a washer, and the upper fork-spring retainer was redesigned. The fork now included a larger 10x13.5-mm oil fill washer, up from 8x11.5 mm.

All 1978 R100RSs were fitted front and rear with "snowflake" cast-alloy wheels. Both were coated with lacquer to make them easier to clean. Fronts were updated with two larger (40x22x7-mm) sealing rings. Rears were all new, featuring a wider, 2.75-inch rim and a drilled 10.24-inch (260-mm) disc brake instead of the Simplex drum brake. The brake disc was supplied by Brembo and

R100RS and /7 Valve Timing, 1978 and Later (2 mm valve clearance, ± 2 degrees)

Model	Intake opening	Intake closing	Exhaust opening	Exhaust closing
R100RS, R100S, R100/7, R80/7, and R75/7	16° BTDC	44° ABDC	56° BBDC	4° ATDC

For 1978 there was a special Motorsport edition of the R100RS. This was primarily for the United States but was also available elsewhere. This publicity example has an oil cooler, generally a 1979 feature, and not indicative of production Motorsport R100RSs. *BMW Mobile Tradition*

featured the holes drilled in a pattern of alternating two holes, rather than twos and threes. Later in the 1978 model year, these Brembo discs were also sometimes fitted to the front wheel.

The rear brake caliper was a twin opposed-piston Brembo, with 38-mm pistons, a superior design to the floating piston design of the front ATE calipers. The rear caliper was mounted on a large alloy plate and attached to a pressed steel brake torque rod. The Brembo rear master cylinder diameter was 15.8 mm. The front brakes were unchanged, and most silver R100RSs retained the blue anodized front brake calipers. On other colored RSs, the front brake calipers were anodized silver.

Several detail changes were made to chassis components for 1978. The fuel tank overflow now included a hose to direct gasoline overflow to the ground in front of the rear wheel instead of on to the engine, as for 1977. While the fairing was much the same, BMW fitted it with a new headlight cover and headlight rubber. The lower side panels that encircled the cylinders were split, so they could be removed without disturbing the exhaust system, and there was an additional metal support bracket. Also new were the handlebar clamps and instrument support, along with a revised instrument-light support and cover. The taillight housing was now flat black, and from May 1978 there was a new rear fender, constructed of foam plastic and painted matte black.

The most noticeable changes were to the instruments. All the MotoMeter instruments now had black faces with green numerals, white needles, and nonreflective glass. There was an electronic (instead of mechanical) tachometer, and an electric quartz clock. A single key now operated the ignition, fuel tank cap, seat lock, and fork lock. On U.S. models the headlight and taillight were wired to turn on with the ignition (there was no headlight "on/off" switch). U.S. models were also inflicted with an annoying turn-signal beeper, wired to the electric start interlock, and loud enough to be comfortably heard at highway speeds. Accompanying this beeper was a change in the turn-signal indicator position to the

R100RS Production 1978 Model Year

Model	Dates	1977	1978	Total
R100RS	08/77-07/78	2,395	4,470	6,865
R100RS	08/77-12/77	751	341	1,092
(United States)	04/78-08/78		4	4
				7,961

top of the warning-light panel. The brake-failure warning light was now at the bottom of the warning-light panel. Completing the ergonomic upgrades were new, softer Magura handgrips.

Other new features included a folding cable lock, stored in the frame backbone tube. The toolkit lacked tire levers because they weren't suitable for use on the softer alloy wheels. All dual seats included the pocket for the first-aid kit, even if the kit wasn't included (as in the United States).

For 1978 BMW offered the R100RS in silver, and metallic gold. The metallic gold RS had black pinstriping and red "R100RS" engine emblems and "1,000 cc" side cover decals. Few original examples have survived, unfortunately, because the paint was exceptionally prone to fading in sunlight. This year also saw the introduction of the Motorsport edition, first of several limited editions. BMW built 200 Motorsports, painted white with orange and blue pinstriping and a red headlight surround. It was available with matching white Krauser saddlebags, and many came with dark blue seat upholstery.

From 1978 the R100RS featured cast-alloy wheels with a rear disc brake. A machined aluminum bracket supported the Brembo rear brake caliper.

1979 R100RS

For the 1979 model year, the M65* engine received its most significant revision. Although the general specifications were unchanged, several subtle updates were made to the camshaft drive, ignition, and drive shaft. These were also shared with the new R45 and R65 boxer twins (see chapter 6).

Engine and Drivetrain

Developments began with the crankcases, which now had black and silver highlighted "BMW" emblems on each side, instead of an emblem indicating a particular model and capacity. The R100RS had new crankcases, not shared with other /7s, but there was a new crankshaft (for all /7s), which incorporated counterweight material riveted to the inner surfaces of the crank webs instead of tungsten plugs. The crankshaft for the 1,000-cc engine was the same as that for the 800-cc, with the same balance factor. The new rear crankshaft seal wasn't as deep as the earlier type.

To eliminate the persistent oil weep from the cylinder base, from May 1979 BMW began fitting

Starting in 1979 the R100RS had an oil cooler, with a solid lower fairing in front of the engine.

A gold R100RS at the press launch in Arizona during 1979. U.S.-specification models like this had reflectors on the fork legs. The rider's attire was strictly 1970s. *Mick Woollett*

a 93x2-mm O-ring to seal the base of each cylinder. During 1979 the oil-filter cartridge was also revised. While the previous type utilized a paper gasket and steel washer, the end of the newer version was crimped to the outer tube and the square section sealing rings glued to the inside of the filter. This was an improvement, as serious engine damage could result if the earlier washer and O-ring weren't correctly fitted. For the R100RS (and R100RT) there was now a specific oil filter with a hinge that provided easier removal and installation with the full fairing.

The R100RS and /7s also received a new camshaft drive with a 50-link single-row 3/8x7/32-inch chain, now with a master link to aid servicing. The drive included a spring-loaded hydraulically damped tensioner. A new front crankshaft bearing cover assisted oil flow to the rear main bearing. The oil pump featured a new inner rotor, and there was a new oil pump pick-up strainer, crankshaft pinion, and cam chain case. The pick-up strainer could no longer split at the spot weld, resulting in obscuring the pick-up hole and blocking the dipstick. The chain case now had ornamental ribbed finning, and there was a new outer cover without any ribbing but incorporating additional side vents. European models now included the new aluminum top engine cover with integral air intake and double-sided crankcase breather that was fitted on U.S. examples during 1978.

The R100RS now included a standard six-row oil cooler, with the outlet connection at the oil filter head, although not all early 1979 R100RSs had the oil cooler. As a prelude to the 1980 model year, U.S. models (from August 1979, number 6 185 422) included another set of Bing carburetors, with revised jetting (165 main jets and 2.66 needle jets) and a new choke housing, new cylinders and pistons, and crankcase breather. As these were essentially 1980 updates, they are described in the next section. All 1979 U.S. R100RSs also had the smaller 38-mm-diameter exhaust header pipes.

One of the main developments was to the ignition, a major update that resulted in a more stable ignition and allowed the bike to be timed while it was running. Although retaining a Bosch contact breaker system, there was now a rotary trigger separately enclosed in a housing within the timing chain cover. The points cam was no longer incorporated as part of the camshaft, but was driven off the end of the camshaft via a self-aligning floating tang and grooved Oldham coupling. This was claimed to isolate the points from camshaft flex and vibration, and it allowed dynamic timing adjustment by rotating the housing while flashing a timing light though the timing hole in the crankcase. A larger breaker-point gap was also specified, with an increased dwell of 120 degrees, and slightly more ignition advance (32 degrees).

BMW also made revisions to the driveshaft to assist gear disengagement. The driveshaft now incorporated a torsional vibrator, consisting of an additional ramped coupling and spring, similar to the one on the transmission input shaft. This was the most effective improvement to the gear shift up to that time. The transmission case also received external vertical cross ribbing for additional strength and heat dissipation.

Chassis

Changes to the chassis were few and relatively minor. Longer shock-absorber mounts on the rear subframe facilitated fitting pannier mounts. The front fork included a new upper triple clamp and fork retainer nut, and a revised clamp secured the instrument panel more rigidly to the top triple clamp. European models now included reflectors on the fork legs like their American counterparts. While the bodywork was as before, a new lower center section for the fairing was necessary to accommodate the oil cooler added during the model year. A solid center panel for the lower fairing with smaller, seven-section grills on each side replaced the open grill. Unfortunately, this sometimes led to a concentration of heat in the front of the engine and diode-board failure. Standard this year was the dual seat, with a new seat cushion and larger black passenger grab rail that included a rack. The solo seat remained an option. BMW offered the R100RS painted in metallic gold or a two-tone blue and silver metallic with red pinstriping. New sidecover decals proclaimed "R100RS" instead of "1,000 cc." These decals were white/red on the blue versions with silver sidecovers. Some bikes had black sidecovers with white decals.

Completing the 1979 upgrades were new handlebar switches, with a more conventional left-side switch for the turn signals, but with an unconventional horn button location above. The Magura handgrips were larger and reshaped. The new taillight housing was black and included two chambers and two bulbs. The price went up to $6,199, but the R100RS was no longer the most expensive BMW motorcycle, as it was usurped by the new R100RT (see chapter 7).

1980 R100RS

Apart from the U.S. versions, the specifications for the 1980 R100RS were similar to those of 1979, and the model carried the same factory code (0377). The years 1978 and 1979 were extremely difficult for BMW, as the company struggled to sell premium motorcycles in the United States in the wake of a falling dollar. With the United States accounting for one-third of sales, the future looked bleak. It was at this time that the company embarked on the change of direction that resulted in both the R80 G/S and K series. In the meantime evolutionary development continued to the M65* engine. From January 1980 the lubrication system was modified with the main front pressure passage to the camshaft altered so as to send oil three ways, first to the new front main bearing bushings and caps, to the camshaft, and then to the rear main bearing. Previously oil was fed initially to the camshaft, then to the front main bearing with the rear main bearing last in the line. Changes to the Bing carburetors included a new top spring for the slide.

BMW also made several modifications to the U.S. models, primarily to allow them to run on low-lead or unleaded regular gasoline, but also to enable the engine to pass more stringent Environmental Protection Agency (EPA) requirements. The combination of high-compression and lower-octane fuel caused detonation on 1979 U.S. models, exacerbated by their high final drive gearing. For 1980 the compression ratio for all U.S. bikes was lowered to 8.2:1. For other countries the compression ratio was unchanged, although European examples were fitted with the crankcase ventilation and air intake of the 1979 U.S. bikes. Lowering compression required new pistons, cylinders, and air intakes. The lower compression ratio was claimed to only slightly reduce the power output, to 67 horsepower at 7,000 rpm.

Official 1980 model year production of U.S. models commenced in November 1979, but all the U.S. R100s received new pistons, cylinder heads, and air intakes from August 1979 (R100RS number 6185422).

BMW also updated the air-box and engine-breather systems on U.S. models to reduce emissions. The new metal top engine cover incorporated 10 grill vents instead of an intake bell, and it had "BMW" cast into each side. There were still three crankcase ventilation hoses, a 10-inch and two shorter hoses with a T-junction. The air filter, and filter box were completely redesigned, with a flat (instead of round) pleated paper filter. The housing itself was sand-cast aluminum and

Other developments for 1979 included a larger rear luggage rack. Most R100RSs by now were fitted with a dual seat.

R100RS Production 1979–80 Model Years

Model	Dates	1978	1979	1980	Total
R100RS	08/78-07/80	704	2,303	2,323	5,330
R100RS (United States)	09/78-07/80	209	223	87	519
R100RS-T (United States)	09/78-06/80	628	656	567	1,851
					7,700

Although the 1981 R100RS looked similar to the 1980 version, there were many improvements. The range of colors was expanded considerably, but the blue example here wasn't so common.

included a top with two snorkel air intakes. Access to the filter was a lot easier than before, as four spring clips located it. The new intake system was intended to lower intake noise while increasing volume, and it was so successful that it was featured, in slightly modified form, on all 1981 engines.

BMW also added a Pulse-Air suction system, similar to one already used by Kawasaki, to pull fresh air into the exhaust port of each cylinder head for the purpose of reducing exhaust emissions. The system consisted of two 10.5-mm-diameter tubes that routed air from a one-way reed valve in the air filter box to a threaded connection to each exhaust port in the cylinder head. It was an endeavor to reduce the level of unburned hydrocarbons by mixing the exhaust gases with clean air, but unfortunately the system caused the annoying side effect of popping during throttle-off deceleration. Hotter spark plugs, Champion N7Y or Bosch W6D, were specified for U.S. models.

While there was little to visually distinguish the 1980 European R100RS from the 1979 version, U.S. models included a few further developments. The choke lever was moved to the clutch-lever bracket on the handlebar because there was no longer room for it on the new air filter box. A new single-cable throttle actuated a junction with separate cables for each carburetor. There were new convex mirrors, the underseat tool tray now had a cover, and finally the annoying turn-signal beepers were omitted. Completing the developments this year was a federally mandated 85-mile-per-hour speedometer.

The combination of another price increase (to $7,025), and less power did little to endear the R100RS to the American buyer, and only a handful of 1980 models were sold in the United States. Not only was it expensive, the venerable M65* engine was struggling to meet noise and emissions requirements while maintaining a suitable power output. The 1980 version was an interim solution until the more efficient A10 engine appeared for 1981. This coincided with a change in U.S. distribution, and in October 1980, BMW North America took over from Butler and Smith.

1981 R100RS

Continual refinement of the 1,000-cc boxer engine saw what was arguably its quintessential development with the A10 engine of 1981. Within the factory walls, the death knell may have already sounded for the large-capacity boxer twin, but this development represented the culmination of a classic design. With significant improvements to the drivetrain and chassis, the R100RS from 1981 until 1984 was arguably the most successful rendition of this fine series. Although the 1977 R100RS, with its elegant touches, was the classic, the 1981–84 R100RS incorporated the finest attributes of this outstanding motorcycle. And while the resurrected R100RS of 1986 provided some improvement, particularly in the chassis, the engine performance and aesthetics weren't comparable to those of the 1981–84 examples. What still hurt the R100RS in 1981 was the price, even though it remained at $7,025.

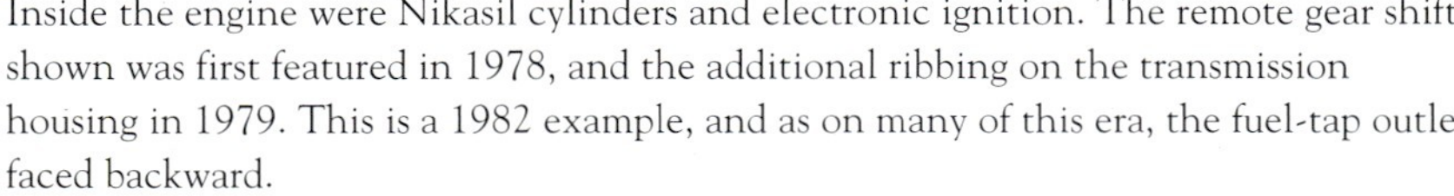
Inside the engine were Nikasil cylinders and electronic ignition. The remote gear shift shown was first featured in 1978, and the additional ribbing on the transmission housing in 1979. This is a 1982 example, and as on many of this era, the fuel-tap outlet faced backward.

The plastic airbox may not have looked as good as the earlier aluminum casting, but it permitted easier access to the air filter.

There were also new 40-mm Bing carburetors from 1981.

U.S. models featured a handlebar-mounted choke from 1980, and this was incorporated on all 1981 models. This switchgear is European specification with a headlight switch.

Engine and Drivetrain

The R100RS received a strengthened engine housing (again not shared with other 1,000-cc versions), modified oilways, and a deeper sump cover with new drain plugs and dipstick. This enlarged the oil capacity to 2.91 quarts (2.75 liters) on the R100RS (with the standard oil cooler).

One of the main updates was new cylinders, Nikasil (by Mahle) or Galnikal (by Kolben Schmidt). Instead of lining aluminum cylinders with cast iron, silicon carbide was applied directly to the aluminum cylinders. The new cylinders only weighed 4.5 pounds (2.025 kilograms), 2.3 pounds (1.035 kilograms) less than before, and their wear qualities were significantly improved. The cylinders were matched to the piston and could no longer be rebored, but with improved heat dissipation, wear was virtually nonexistent. Liquid sealant was no longer used at the base of the cylinder (although the O-ring was retained), and the protective tube pushrod rings were now soldered to the cylinders.

New for 1981 was a lighter pressure die-cast rear drive housing.

There was no shortage of warning decals on the R100RS, and European models included this first-aid-kit decal.

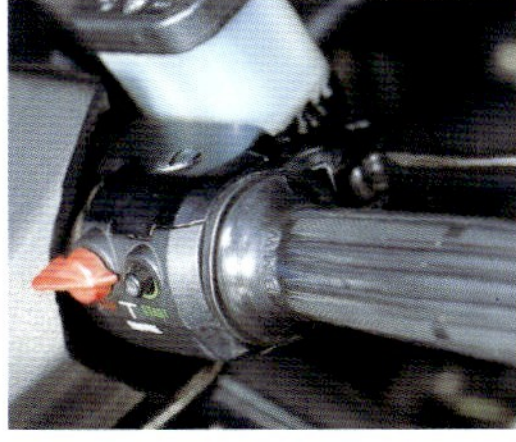

Another improvement was the relocation of the front brake master cylinder to the right handlebar.

One of the most significant improvements for 1981 was to the front braking system, with twin Brembo brake calipers replacing the floating ATE calipers. The cast-alloy front wheel rim was also slightly wider.

R100RS Carburetors (1981–84)

Left Carburetor	Bing 94/40/111 (113 U.S. models)
Right Carburetor	Bing 94/40/112 (114 U.S. models)
Main Jet	160
Needle Jet	2.66
Jet Needle No.	46-341
Needle Position	3 (2 U.S. models)
Idle Jet	45

The rear cylinder studs were now the same length as the front (11.895 inches or 305 mm), and the piston-pin offset from the centerline was reduced to 1.0 mm (from 1.5 mm). While European examples retained the 9.5:1 compression ratio, producing the same 70 horsepower but at a slightly lower 7,000 rpm, U.S. models were still running 8.2:1, but there was no claimed power figure.

The crankshaft was unchanged but for a new lock ring and thrust washer for the substantially lighter pressed-steel (rather than billet-cast) flywheel. This was more like a three-spoked cross with riveted ring starter gear. The flywheel O-ring was now inside the flywheel cap.

There were also new cylinder heads, with new and narrower exhaust valve seats (reduced from 2.0 mm to 1.5 mm. Unfortunately, valve recession became more of a problem after this change, particularly in the United States with its lead-free gasoline.

The crankcase ventilation on all 1981 models was now the same revised double-sided breather that first appeared on U.S. examples for 1979. This included the new, vented top engine cover, and there was a revised chain-case cover (to accommodate the new ignition), now with black highlighting between the ornamental finning, previously reserved for the smaller R65.

The new 40-mm Bing carburetors included a more positive locator for the throttle slides, with a supplementary piston guideway. All 1981 models were fitted with the rectangular pleated-paper air filter and airbox design first used on 1980 U.S. models, except that the body and top were now black plastic, instead of cast aluminum, with two removable forward-facing plastic snorkels. The smoother plastic finish was claimed to reduce turbulence and restriction, permitting leaner jetting. The air filter housing was now plastic rather than rubber, and the new setup permitted easier access to the filter.

U.S. versions retained the Pulse-Air emissions system, but it now incorporated a vacuum shutoff connected to the reed valve inside the air box to eliminate the annoying popping on the overrun. This system resulted in improved cold-weather performance and throttle response throughout the rev range, because the carburetion didn't need to be as lean.

All RSs for 1981 had the choke lever on the clutch-lever perch. The Magura throttle assembly retained the excellent cam and chain system, but was the type fitted to U.S. models in 1980, with a single cable now connecting to a junction block and two cables running to each carburetor to reduce friction. This throttle lacked a stop.

For the exhaust, using 38x1.5-mm exhaust pipes and an additional rear crossover balance pipe behind the sump helped broaden the powerband. Also new were the exhaust spider nuts and a pair of more efficient mufflers, with specific mufflers for the United States.

Experience with the smaller R65 had shown the benefits of a lighter clutch and flywheel, especially in combination with the driveshaft shock absorber, and this was passed onto the A10 engine. The weight of the flywheel and clutch assembly was reduced by 40 percent, to less than 10 pounds, with a resulting vast improvement in throttle response. Part of the weight savings was from a new, thinner plate, with a much stronger diaphragm spring, and spring plate. This new clutch was accompanied by a new operating mechanism, running in ball and needle bearings. This included a new pushrod, clutch piston, and gearbox-end clutch lever, and resulted in a 30 percent reduction in draw effort.

BMW updated the transmission with a new mainshaft, drive pinion and seal, input shaft, rear transmission cover, kickstart ratio and spline for the still-optional kickstart, and Heim joints for the gear shift mechanism. Transmission ratios were unchanged. BMW also revised the shock absorber on the driveshaft and the output needle bearing (now a 15x30x18 mm instead of 15x32x17 mm) for the pinion gear in the final drive. There was also a new hose clip for the driveshaft gaiter, and the rear drive casting was a new, lighter, and stronger pressure die casting similar to that designed for the monoshock R80 G/S.

Electrical System and Ignition

Developments to the electrical system began with all R100s for 1981 incorporating the more powerful Bosch G 1 14V 20A 280-watt alternator, a new microelement electronic Wehrle E1951B/14V voltage regulator to improve charging, and a 0.7-kilowatt Bosch starter motor. One of the most practical updates was the Bosch TSZH electronic ignition. This transistorized, breakerless system used a Hall-effect trigger with integral centrifugal advance, and new lighter 6-volt coils, but the timing (advance from 1,550–3,000 rpm with 32 degrees maximum) was unchanged. The spark plugs for all non-U.S. 1,000-cc models were Bosch W5D, Beru 14-5D, or Champion N6Y for Europe. U.S. models were

Changes to the instrument panel for 1981 included an electronic tachometer and a revised warning-light display.

Despite the improvements to the engine and chassis for 1981, the cockpit remained familiar and still included the adjustable steering damper.

By 1982 the R100RS may have been six years old, but it was still a wonderfully effective sport-touring motorcycle. This example (number 6392852) is original and unrestored.

R100RSs with dual seats always featured special model emblems.

fitted with Bosch W6D, Beru 14-6D, or Champion N7Y. Also new were the BMW Mareg 28-Ah battery and Hella TBB 53 turn signals.

Chassis

Although there were some changes to the frame and swingarm for 1981, rake was still 28.5 degrees with 95 mm (3.7 inches) of trail. To improve access to the battery, there was a new rear subframe. Following its experience in developing the Monolever R80 G/S, BMW added an additional cylindrical brace to the swingarm. The swingarm was also given new pivot pins, seal rings, and tapered roller bearings. The bearings were changed again in January 1981. All 1981 R100RSs included a warning plate regarding the transistorized ignition, and from April 1981 BMW began fitting new chassis identification plates.

Although the cast-aluminum "snowflake" wheels looked similar to earlier wheels, the front wheel was now a wider 2.15Bx19-inch, but the tire size (3.25Hx19) was unchanged. The rear wheel remained a 2.75Bx18-inch with a 4.00Hx18 tire.

The Sachs-built front fork was new, with shorter fork springs (21.22 inches or 539 mm) of

With the K100 intended to replace the R100, there were several final limited editions of the R100RS. This is one of the final European Classic Series 500 of 1984. U.S. final editions were white.

a thicker wire diameter (0.167 inch or 4.25 mm), new dampers, and new fork legs that were cast to accept rectangular reflectors. Each leg also required less fluid (0.22 cc), and fork travel was unchanged. On some R100RSs this year, the fork legs weren't black, but plain alloy, although most examples still had the black fork legs. During 1981 (from number 6077830), the fork design was changed to include an additional compression coil spring at the base of the damping rod. Although the rear Boge shock absorbers were unchanged, the self-leveling Nivomat units of the R100RT were an option.

BMW greatly improved the front brakes by fitting 38-mm opposed-piston Brembo calipers, asbestos-free pads, and a new, bar-mounted master cylinder. Diameter of the perforated front brake disc was now quoted at 260 mm. Wet-weather braking was claimed to be 40 percent improved. The master cylinder piston diameter was 15 mm, or sometimes 16 mm, and the front brake lines included a T-junction with pressure switch located on the lower triple clamp. The same Brembo disc as before was at the rear, but with the smaller 14-mm master cylinder of the 1979 R100S, providing an improved leverage ratio.

There was no change to the bodywork, but the front fender received a new metal brace with shorter mounting bolts. A longer front fender was still an option. The RS was offered in smoke black or red (without pinstriping) with white "R100RS" sidecover decals. The John Player Special was a limited edition in black with gold wheels and decals, released to coincide with the racing 6-series JPS cars.

Each Classic Series came with this numbered plaque. A tiny stamp indicates this is number 362, but you have to look closely to see it.

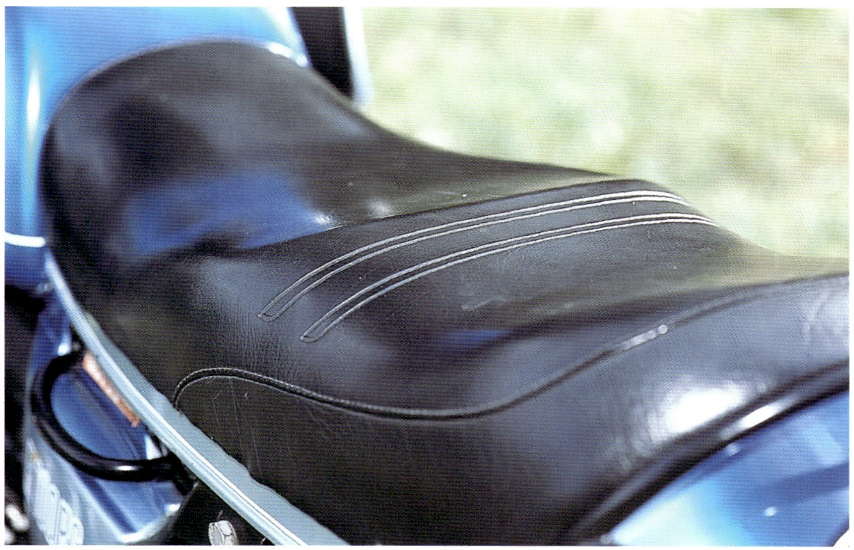

The Classic Series also included a unique seat.

After 1982 the optional panniers were this boxier BMW type, and for the Classic Series they were painted silver.

A tinted windshield was standard on the Classic Series. All lower fairings from 1978 were split to allow easier removal.

Although the speedometer, headlight, and taillight were unchanged, there was a new electronic tachometer, with the rpm indication on the lower face. On the new instrument-light support, a "High Beam" warning light at the bottom replaced "Brake Failure." U.S. versions still had the ridiculous 85-mile-per-hour speedometer and hard-wired headlight.

The R100RS retained the two-stage hydraulic steering damper, and after years of complaint, BMW finally redesigned side and centerstands, with rubber plugs on the base of the centerstand. The sidestand was no longer self-retracting. Along with a new rear turn-signal bracket, footpeg mounts were redesigned to reduce vibration, with a slightly higher and more rearward location. There was a recall early in 1981 to replace the right-side footpeg, as its location could prevent ease of operation of the rear brake. Passenger footpegs were now adjustable. While the remote gear shift linkage was similar to the previous version, there was no longer a grease nipple at the pivot.

1982 R100RS

With most of its developmental resources going into the forthcoming K series, BMW made few changes to the R100RS for 1982. The engine was as before, but from January 1982, a revised frame and centerstand were fitted, and beginning April 1, the R100RS had a new transmission input helical gear and a new fifth gear.The one-key lock was a new pattern this year, and U.S. R100RSs from number 6226150 also received new rear turn-signal brackets.

During 1982 many of the Karcoma (but not Germa) fuel petcocks were changed with the feed angling backward instead of down, to clear the throttle and choke cables. The optional 40-liter pannier bags were a new rectangular style with an improved latch location to the frame mount. The panniers were standard equipment in the United States, but the price of the R100RS was unchanged at $7,025. Several other colors were now available, and for the European market, BMW offered an optional mother-of-pearl metallic white with red pinstriping. A numbered limited-edition R100RSR, primarily for the Japanese market, was offered in black with white and red pinstripes.

1983–84 R100RS

As the R100RS drew toward its demise, there was inevitably little development made during the final two years. From May 1983 there was a new air filter top for all twins, and from March 1983 the final drive included an additional locating

The silver and blue colors of the final twin-shock R100RS Classic Series bikes were chosen to create an association with the first edition.

dowel. There was a new wiring harness for 1983, and modifications to the pannier latches and keys. Changes to the gearbox included an improved gear selector cam plate, with deepened detent valleys to eliminate false neutrals. First featured on the R80ST (chapter 8), this could also be fitted to all earlier twins from 1969. The year 1983 also saw the return of the 140-mile-per-hour speedometer on U.S. examples. The price decreased to $6,590, but for 1984 rose again to $6,990. During 1984, in response to wheels cracking, the cast wheels included additional support material around the spokes.

With the K100 series about to supplant the R100, there were two 1984 final limited editions, supposedly the last of the line. For Europe there was a numbered Series 500 in blue and silver, with a numbered plaque on each side of the fairing, a thicker seat with new upholstery, tinted windscreen, and matching silver panniers. In the U.S. market, BMW offered 250 final editions in white, with red and blue pinstripes, panniers, standard single and dual seats, and a BMW System II helmet.

These final editions were meant to be the final breath for the R100RS, but pressure from enthusiasts saw it resurrected only two years later in Monolever form. The new R100RS was for many but a pale imitation of the original. It was no longer the ground-breaking exotic motorcycle that stunned the world in 1976, but an outdated throwback that further enhanced the appeal of the twin-shock versions.

After 1982, the cast wheels incorporated additional strengthening to prevent breakage.

R100RS Dimensions, Weights, and Performance (1981–84)

Overall width	29.37 inches
Saddle height	32.3 inches
Overall length	87.0 inches
Overall height	51.2 inches
Wheelbase	57.7 inches
Weight including oil but without fuel	463 pounds
Weight including oil and fuel	507 pounds
Top speed	Over 124 mph
0-400 meters	13.2 seconds

R100RS Production 1981–84 Model Years

Model	Dates	1980	1981	1982	1983	1984	Total
R100RS	09/80-10/84	1,073	3,907	3,748	2,263	42	11,033
R100RS (United States)	09/80-10/84	256	860	215	772	284	2,387
							13,420

Chapter 6

R100S, R100/7, R100T, R80/7, R75/7, and R60/7 (1977–80)

The R100S was a continuation of the styling of the R90S. Although supplanted by the R100RS at the top of the range, the R100S was the fastest model in the lineup. It was relatively popular in the United States in 1977 and 1978, but 1979 examples like this are rare.

Alongside the R100RS for 1977 was a completely new range, the /7 series. Now comprising five models, replacing the successful four-model range of the R90S and /6, the displacement for the top models jumped to the 980 cc of the R100RS. The 900-cc models were discontinued, and initially, the 750- and 600-cc versions were much as before, in updated form. The R100S and R100/7 were updates of the R90S and R90/6, with the 980-cc engine. As in the past there was a high degree of model uniformity and parts interchangeability, with all /7s sharing much with the more expensive R100RS. The R75/7 was short lived, replaced by the slightly larger R80/7 for 1978, and the R60/7 was effectively replaced by the new R65 at the end of 1978. There were also other transitory variations on the /7 theme, some specifically for the U.S. market, such as the R100S Touring, and similar R100T, as the R100/7 was especially popular in the United States.

1977 R100S, R100/7, R75/7, and R60/7

The R100S continued the style of its illustrious predecessor, the R90S. It was also an improved motorcycle, even if it lacked the R90S mystique. And despite slightly lower power output, the R90S was arguably the strongest performer in the 1977 lineup. The other /7s also incorporated many of the improvements introduced on the R100RS.

/7 Chassis Numbers

Type	Numbers	Model Year	Production Dates
R60/7	6000001 to 6007000	1977	09/76– 08/77
R60/7	6007001 to 6012000	1978	09/77–08/78
R60/7	6015001 to 6016000	1979	09/78–08/80
R60/7 (United States)	6100001 to 6101000	1977	09/76–08/77
R60/7 (United States)	6101001 to 6102000	1978	09/77–08/78
R75/7	6020001 to 6025000	1977	09/76–08/77
R75/7	6220001 to 6222000	1978	09/77–08/78
R75/7	6222001 to 6223000	1979	09/78–08/80
R75/7 (United States)	6120001 to 6121474	1977	09/76–08/77
R80/7	6025001 to 6030000	1978	09/77–08/78
R80/7	6030001 to 6034000	1979	09/78–08/80
R80/7 (United States)	6122501 to 6124909	1978	09/77–08/78
R80/7 (United States)	6126001 to 6128000	1979	09/78–08/80
R100/7	6040001 to 6045000	1977	09/76–08/77
R100/7	6045001 to 6050000	1978	09/77–08/78
R100/7 (United States)	6140001 to 6144251	1977	09/76–08/77
R100/7 (United States)	6145001 to 6148196	1978	09/77–08/78
R100/7 (United States)	6170001 to 6172000	1979	09/78–08/80
R100T	6050001 to 6054000	1979	09/78–08/80
R100T (United States)	6103001 to 6104000	1979	09/78–08/80
R100S	6060001 to 6065000	1977	09/76–08/77
R100S	6065001 to 6070000	1978	09/77–08/78
R100S	6070001 to 6073000	1979	09/78–08/80
R100S (United States)	6160001 to 6161385	1977	09/76– 08/77
R100S (United States)	6162501 to 6163870	1978	09/77–08/78
R100S (United States)	6165001 to 6167000	1979	09/78–08/80

Although the R80/7 replaced the R75/7 for 1978, the two models were visually similar. All U.S. models came with fork-leg reflectors and round reflectors at the rear, and a single front disc brake was standard. This is a period photo of a 1978 R80/7. *Cycle World*

/7 Engine Specifications 1977–78

Model	Bore (mm)	Stroke (mm)	Capacity (cc)	Compression Ratio	Horsepower DIN
R60/7	73.5	70.6	599	9.2:1	40@6400 rpm
R75/7	82	70.6	745	9.0:1	50@6200 rpm
R100/7	94	70.6	980	9.1:1	60@6500 rpm
R100S	94	70.6	980	9.5:1	65@6600 rpm

Engine

As with the /6 series, each model of the /7 series represented a slightly different variation on the Type 247/76 engine theme. There was basically no difference inside the engine of the R60/7 and R75/7 and their respective /6 variants. The R100/7 engine was also similar to that of the R90/6. There were still only two camshafts, with the R60/7 receiving the milder 284-degree camshaft and all other models the 308-degree camshaft. The R100S engine was identical in specification to the R100RS engine, although the S's power output was slightly less, due to a more restrictive exhaust system. The quoted weight of the /7 engines was identical to their respective /6 variants.

Inside the cylinder head of the R60/7, the 38- and 34-mm valves were the same as the R60/6 (and R60/5), and the 42- and 38-mm valves of the R75/7 were unchanged from the earlier 750. While the R100/7 valves were the 42- and 40-mm of the R90/6, the R100S featured the 44-mm inlet and 40-mm exhaust valves of the R100RS. The engine breather system on the R75/7, R100/7, and R100S was the updated setup of the R100RS, while the R60/7 retained the /6 engine-breather housing. All models featured the new angular rocker covers, plain aluminum cylinders, and a specific black model-identification emblem on the engine cases. The R100S emblem was highlighted in red to match the bodywork, and this model also featured black anodized valve covers like those of the R100RS.

The R75/7 and R100/7 retained the 36x25-mm intake manifolds from the /6, with the R100S

R100S, R100/7, R75/7, and R60/7 Carburetors

	R60/7	R75/7	R100/7	R100S
Left Carburetor	Bing 1/26/123	Bing 64/32/13	Bing 64/32/19	Bing 94/40/103
Right Carburetor	Bing 1/26/124	Bing 64/32/14	Bing 64/32/20	Bing 94/40/104
Main Jet	140	145	150	170
Needle Jet	2.68	2.66	2.68	2.66
Jet Needle No.	46-234	46-241	46-241	46-341
Needle Position	2	3	3	3
Idle Jet	40	50	50	45

All /7s had a single Fiamm horn, mounted on the left underneath the fuel tank.

The /7 seat was shorter, but otherwise the same as that of the final /6.

/7 Final Drive Ratios

	Number of Teeth	Ratio (optional)
R60/7	11:37	1:3.36 (1:3.56)
R75/7	10:32	1:3.2 (1:3.36)
R100/7	11:34	1:3.09 (1:3.2)
R100S, R100/7 US	11:32	1:2.91 (1:3.0)

sharing its 40-mm manifolds with the R100RS. While the R100RS also received 40-mm diameter exhaust header pipes, the R100S, R100/7, R75/7, and R60/7 continued with 38x1.5-mm exhaust headers. Exhaust and carburetion were essentially carried over from the previous models, except that the R100S used Bing 94 carburetors similar to those on the R100RS.

Clutch and Final Drive

All /7s featured the revised clutch and flywheel with different starter ratio of the R100RS, with the R100S and R100/7 clutch spring also 2.8-mm. The R75/5 and R60/7 had a 2.6-mm spring. A different final drive ratio for each version also distinguished the /7, with the U.S. R100/7 having a higher 1:3.0 ratio than European versions.

Electrical System and Ignition

While the R100S shared the smaller 250-watt Bosch G1 14V 18A 22/240W alternator with the R100RS, all other /7s featured the Bosch G1 14V 20A 21/280 W alternator of the R90/6, R75/6, and R60/6. Also featured on all /7s was the 0.6-horsepower Bosch starter motor and 28-Ah Varta battery. Spark plug leads and caps were new, and spark plugs were generally warmer. These were Bosch W225 T30, Beru 230/14/3A, or Champion N6Y spark plugs for the R100S and R60/7, with Bosch W200 T30, Beru 200/14/3A, or Champion N7Y spark plugs for the R100/7 and R75/7.

The touring /7 for 1977 and 1978 featured wire-spoked wheels and aluminum rims. The fork legs were plain aluminum, and the touring models included fork gaiters. Dual front discs were an option, and the silver-anodized brake calipers indicate this is a 1978 model.

Chassis

All the /7s shared frame Type 247/77, with additional strengthening, including the additional brace between the front frame downtubes, with the R100RS. Also shared was the suspension. Unlike the R100RS that had black fork legs, all /7 fork legs and those on the R100S, were plain aluminum. The fork springs were longer at 22.32 inches (567 mm), and the steering lock was 42 degrees to each side. The R100S retained the more sporting rubber fork cups, with gaiters still featured on other /7s. There was a new, polished steel upper triple clamp, and black anodized handlebar clamps. The rear Boge shock absorbers no longer had alloy covers over the black springs.

All the wheels for 1977 /7s and R100Ss were wire spoked, as on the /6 models, with aluminum rims and 40 chrome-plated spokes. Only the 1,000-cc models received H-rated tires (up to 130 miles per hour). Except for the R60/7, the front brakes were the same as those of the 1976 /6s, the R100S retaining dual perforated front discs, and all /7s a single front disc brake. The Duplex drum brake that had featured on the first /5 was no longer specified. The 40-mm ATE front brake calipers were black anodized. All models had a Simplex rear drum brake.

A 23.4-inch (600-mm) chrome-plated tubular-steel handlebar was standard, but U.S. /7s had a broader, 26.52-inch (680-mm) handlebar. The frame modifications improved stability, so a steering damper was not standard on the R100S and /7s, although this was an option. As on the /6, the round mirrors were black on the R100S and chrome-plated on other /7s. An additional frame brace was now where the horn was previously located, so the earlier feeble Bosch horn was

/7 Production 1977 Model

Model	Dates	1976	1977	Total
R60/7	08/76–07/77	2,207	3,310	5,517
R60/7 (United States)	08/76–06/77	296	111	407
R75/7	08/76–07/77	1,533	2,974	4,507
R75/7 (United States)	08/76–06/77	1,315	159	1,474
R100/7	08/76–07/77	1,771	1,643	3,414
R100/7 (United States)	08/76–07/77	1,587	864	2,451
R100S	08/76–06/77	1,461	1,688	3,149
R100S (United States)	08/76–06/77	841	544	1,385
				22,304

replaced with a new Fiamm 410-Hz horn on the left. The twin horns of the R100RS were an option.

Ostensibly the /7 was very similar to the /6, but all models and the R100S now shared the sporting 24-liter fuel tank and front fender of the R90S. The lockable fuel filler cap was flush mounted as on the R100RS. The lower brace from the front fender was omitted, although the fork-leg casting still retained the mount, even on the RS. The rear fender was painted to match the fuel tank on /7s, but black on the R100S. Pinstriping on /7s encircled the side of the tank. Pinstriping on the R100S was more abbreviated, as on the R90S and R100RS. The handlebar-mounted fairing of the R100S was identical to that of the R90S, as was the dual seat (but with a black grab handle). The left-side handle was also black on the R100S; it was chrome on other /7s. The R100S also had black sidecovers, with gold "1,000 cc" decals, and the only color for the R100S for 1977 was metallic red with gold pinstriping. Three colors were specified for the other /7s: Avus black, metallic blue, and metallic red. The /7 dual seat was similar to that of the 1975 and 1976 /6, with cross pleating and a chrome grab rail. The lower metal fixtures were now black rather than chrome, and there was a round BMW emblem on the tail, along with a specific decal model emblem. The /7s also had the new style rectangular footpeg rubbers.

The instruments and instrument layout were identical to that of the final /6, and the handlebar switches were the same as those of the R100RS, with additional wings for the turn-signal and high-beam switches. The ignition switch remained on the left headlight bracket on the R100S and /7s. As always, the list of options was extensive, ranging from a kickstart and oil cooler, to touring fairing and heavy-duty suspension.

R100S, R100/7, R75/7 and R60/7 Dimensions, Weights and Performance

Type	R100S	R100/7	R75/7	R60/7
Overall width	29.37 inches	29.37 inches	29.37 inches	29.37 inches
Saddle height	32.3 inches	31.9 inches	31.9 inches	31.9 inches
Overall length	85.8 inches	85.8 inches	85.8 inches	85.8 inches
Overall height	47.6 inches	42.5 inches	42.5 inches	42.5 inches
Wheelbase	57.7 inches	57.7 inches	57.7 inches	57.7 inches
Weight including oil but without fuel	441 pounds	430 pounds	430 pounds	430 pounds
Weight including oil and fuel	485 pounds	474 pounds	474 pounds	474 pounds
Top speed	Over 124 mph	117 mph	110 mph	104 mph
0–100 mph	12.6 seconds	13.7 seconds	19.8 seconds	27.5 seconds

1978 R100S, R100/7, R80/7, and R60/7

For 1978 BMW replaced the R75/7 with a new model, the R80/7, although a few R75/7s were produced as 1978 models for Europe. The R80/7 was very similar to the R75/5, but for 2.8-mm-larger pistons and cylinders, and the engine type was known as the M85*. BMW also offered a lower compression version (8:1, 50 horsepower), but this wasn't sold in the United States. The valve sizes were unchanged, and the claimed weight for the 800-cc engine (with starter, carburetor, and oil) was slightly less than for the 750, at 140 pounds (63.5 kilograms). The R60/7 was proving unpopular in the United States, so only a small number were produced toward the end of 1977, as 1978 models. This year also saw a variety of additional official, police, and touring models, the R60/7 T, the R80/7 T, and R80/7 N.

All /7s included the developments already detailed for the R100RS. In the engine this included a double-sided engine breather on U.S. examples from R80/7 number 6124338, R100/7 number 6147574, and R100S number 6163465, along with a new top engine cover. The R100S, R100/7, and R80/7 were fitted with a new camshaft, and the R80/7 was the first model to feature Seeger-style wrist pin circlips. The R80/7 also used the 2.6-mm clutch diaphragm spring, and while the electrical and ignition system was unchanged, there were much warmer Bosch W175 T30, Beru 175/14/3A, or Champion N10Y spark plugs. The R60/7 also received a new camshaft, providing the same duration as before but advanced 6 degrees. There was a new type of flat-topped Bing carburetor for the R80/7, without a spring seating the throttle valve. During 1978 the U.S. R100S (from number

There were slightly different handlebar switches for 1977, with a wing extension for the thumb.

The right switch block included an extension for improved turn-signal selection. These switches lasted through 1978.

R80/7 Engine Specifications

Bore (mm)	Stroke (mm)	Capacity (cc)	Compression Ratio	Power (DIN)
84.8	70.6	797	9.2:1	55@7000 rpm

R80/7 Carburetors

Left Carburetor	Bing 64/32/201
Right Carburetor	Bing 64/32/202
Main Jet	145
Needle Jet	2.66
Jet Needle No.	46-241
Needle Position	3
Idle Jet	50

R80/7 Dimensions, Weights and Performance

Overall width	29.37 inches
Saddle height	31.9 inches
Overall length	85.8 inches
Overall height	42.5 inches
Wheelbase	57.7 inches
Weight including oil but without fuel	430 pounds
Weight including oil and fuel	474 pounds
Top speed	113 mph
0–100 mph	15.6 seconds

New for 1978 was the R80/7. This early example has /6 rocker covers and is fitted out with a number of factory optional accessories. These include the Krauser panniers, windshield, kickstart, driving lights, second front disc, and instruments.

The Bing carburetors on early R80/7s featured flat tops, and the R80/7 was the only model to include this type of carburetor.

From 1978, all R100Ss had cast wheels with a rear disc brake and Brembo twin-piston brake caliper.

1978 Final Drive Ratios

	Number of Teeth	Ratio
(optional)		
R80/7	10:32	1:3.20 (1:3.36)
R80/7 (low compression)	11:37	1:3.36
R60/7	9:32	1:3.56

6163465) also received the Bing carburetors with leaner jetting. The gear shift pivoted from the footpeg with a linkage this year.

BMW revised the R60/7's final drive ratio for 1978. All U.S. R80/7s up to number 6 124 337 were fitted with the 1:3.36 ratio. Starting with number 6 124 338 they had the 1:3.20 ratio. Starting with number 6 147 575, BMW changed the R100/7 U.S. final drive ratio to the 1:3.09 of the European models, accompanied by a W=1.144 speedometer.

Most of the chassis updates for 1978 were also shared with the R100RS. While the first 1978 R100Ss had wire-spoked wheels and a drum rear brake, early in the model year BMW began substituting the cast wheels and Brembo rear disc brake of the R100RS. The R100/7, R80/7, and R60/7 continued with the spoked wheels and a rear drum brake, but there was also a special R100/7 for the United States with the alloy wheels and a rear drum brake. These were the same wheels originally offered for the 1977 R100RS and were a precursor to those fitted to the R100T in 1979. Both cast and wire wheels this year included two new larger seals, so the hub for the spoked wheel was new. On all U.S. R100/7, R80/7, and R60/7 models, there was only a single front disc brake, although European R100/7 and R80/7s featured a second front disc. On European /7s the cast-alloy wheels and rear disc brake (of the R100RS and R100S) were also an option this year. R100/7 and R100S forks were updated with new damper rods like those fitted to the R100RS. All the ATE front brake calipers for the R100S and /7s were anodized silver rather than black.

/7 Production 1978 Model Year

Model	Dates	1977	1978	Total
R60/7 and R60/7T	07/77–07/78	3,035	1,391	4,426
R60/7 (United States)	08/77–12/77	158		158
R75/7	08/77–05/78	107	171	278
R80/7, R80/7N, and R80/7T	07/77–07/78	2,323	3,658	5,981
R80/7 (United States)	08/77–03/78	1,813	596	2,409
R100/7	07/77–07/78	898	2,185	3,083
R100/7 (United States)	07/77–07/78	2,565	631	3,196
R100S	07/77–07/78	752	3,003	3,755
R100S (United States)	07/77–07/78	963	407	1,370
				24,656

There were new instruments, with green lettering for 1978. This R100S has an incorrect voltmeter.

During the year the front brake discs were changed to the Brembo rear disc type, with a different drilled pattern of holes.

There were a few changes to the equipment for 1978. Numerals on the instruments were now painted green, and there was a single key system for the four locks. Unfortunately this still didn't work satisfactorily, as some of the supplied keys wouldn't operate all the locks. U.S. models had the loud turn-signal beepers, and the R100S and all /7s featured a vinyl-covered foam pad over the new upper triple clamp. From May 1978, all /7s received a new rear fender. The R100S now had twin Fiamm horns like the R100RS, and a cable lock in the backbone frame tube.

In addition to all the regular models, many specials were offered for 1978. A special U.S. model R100S lacked the handlebar fairing but had higher R100/7 handlebars and the clock and voltmeter housed in accessory pods. This also came with the option of a touring package that included a Luftmeister fairing and Krauser luggage. Another special edition was the R100S Motorsport, a rather mysterious model sometimes referred to as the R100SRS, as it was marketed under this designation in the United Kingdom, where most were sold. These featured the 70-horsepower R100RS engine, but with a smaller S handlebar fairing. The colors were identical to the similar R100RS Motorsport, and equipment extended to single and dual seats, engine protection bars, and a kilometers-per-hour speedometer (with a miles-per-hour speedometer in a separate box). This indicated the model was originally intended for another market, possibly Australia.

The range of colors was expanded for 1978, with the R100S now available in a metallic dark red with gold pinstriping. The "1,000 cc" side cover decals were red. The /7 was available in metallic black, blue, or orange, with tank pinstripes as before. Also available for 1978 was a metallic red, with R100S-style gold pinstriping and black side covers and rear fender. The optional engine protection bars and luggage racks were also now black instead of chrome.

The R100S seat was the same as that of the R90S, but with "100S" emblems. The dual-bulb taillight was fitted from 1979 through 1984.

1979 R100S, R100T, R100/7, R80/7, and R60/7

With the release of the R65, the R60/7 disappeared from the U.S. lineup for 1979, although it was produced in small quantities for other markets through 1980. There were now five 1,000-cc models (including the RS and RT), with the new R100T filling a void as a touring machine between the sporting R100S and basic R100/7. The R100T specification also varied between markets, but in the United States it featured standard chrome saddlebag brackets and engine protection bars, voltmeter, quartz clock, an electrical accessory outlet, and rear mud flap. Despite its high specification

For 1979 the R100S received the 70-horsepower engine of the R100RS, with 40-mm exhaust header pipes. All engines had "BMW" emblems instead of individual model designation badges. Twin Fiamm horns were standard on the R100S from 1978.

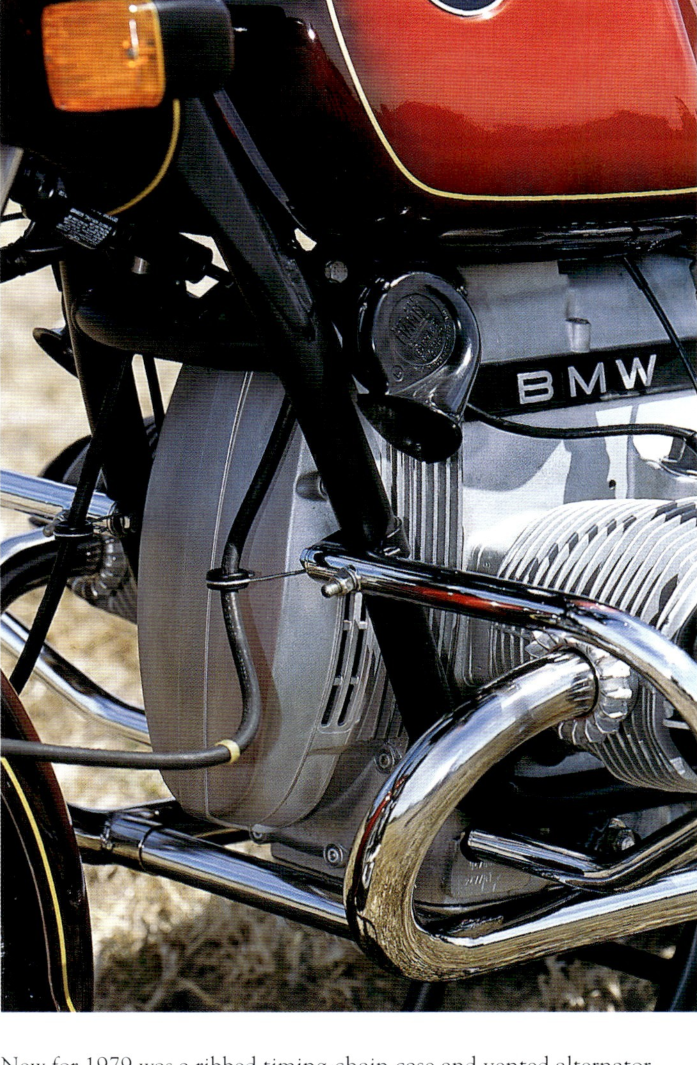

New for 1979 was a ribbed timing-chain case and vented alternator cover. Underneath the cover was a single-row timing chain and new contact-breaker assembly. One of the improvements of the /7 over the /6 was the brace between the two front frame downtubes. The steering damper was an option on the R100S.

Instead of the 38-mm Dell'Orto carburetors of the R90S, the R100S had 40-mm Bing CV carburetors. The remote gear shift linkage featured from 1978, and originally included a rubber bellows over the rod and joints. There was also a grease nipple at the pivot. The 1979 versions like this incorporated additional external transmission case webbing.

and keen pricing ($1,415 less than the R100RT), the R100T sold in very limited numbers.

All 1979 1,000-cc models included the updates already detailed for the R100RS, but the R100S now featured the more powerful R100RS engine with the same Bing 94/40/105 and 106 carburetors, and 40-mm exhaust header pipes. The R100T and R100/7 engine was that of the previous R100S (with 40-mm intake manifolds and Bing 40-mm carburetors) and also included the 40-mm exhaust pipes. The rocker covers were aluminum colored rather than black. Also like the R100RS, the R100T and R100/7 now used the smaller alternator and Bosch W225 T30 or W6D, Beru 200/14/3A, or Champion N7Y spark plugs.

The 1,000-cc engines now had 44-mm inlet and 40-mm exhaust valves, but U.S. 1,000-cc models featured different cylinder heads with valve seats supposedly more suitable for use with low-lead gasoline. The engine breather on all /7s was now the double-sided type, with a new top engine cover with integral air intake. U.S. models included a different cover with slotted grill intake. These developments didn't feature on the U.S. R80/7s until number 6 126 147. They then included new cylinder heads, the revised intake and breather setup, and new carburetors (64/32/321 and 322). From August 1979 all the R80/7 carburetors were changed back to the domed-top type, with cylinder base O-rings from May 1979. All U.S. R100s had the 2.91 final drive, with a W=1.078 speedometer. The U.S. R80/7 final drive was 1:3.20, and the final drive for the European R100T was 1:3.0.

From August 1979, starting with U.S. R100/7, number 6 170 415 and U.S. R100S number 6 165 103, several updates were intended for U.S. models in the 1980 model year. These included new Bing carburetors with 165 main jets, cylinders, pistons, air filter, the Pulse-Air air injection system with inserts in the cylinder head, and a new breather.

There were no fork gaiters on any models for 1979, all forks featuring the sleeves with felt seals of the R100RS and R100S. Setting the R100S apart were black fork legs, and European models now included the side reflectors previously reserved for U.S. models. Standard on all /7s were twin front discs and cast-alloy wheels. As before, the R100S retained a rear disc brake and 2.75-inch rim, while the R100T, R100/7 and R80/7 had the Simplex drum brake with 2.50-inch rear rim. The R100S received a new rear axle, the same as that for the R100RS, and a smaller diameter (14-mm) master cylinder for the rear disc brake.

This year the standard seat for the R100T, R100/7, and R80/7 was the same type as that of the R100S, with a fiberglass base and tail section. This seat included a larger black grab rail and a new seat cushion, but the older style seat was still available. The R100T had special colors (red metallic/silver metallic) paintwork, with silver sidecovers, while all other /7s were now with black sidecovers. The range of colors available was now considerably expanded. One color offered only in the United States was Havana gold. The sidecover decals indicated the model type and engine displacement.

Other updates included new handlebar switches, twin Fiamm horns on all 1,000-cc models, and the new twin-bulb taillight assembly. U.S. R100/7s and R80/7s also featured the broader, 27-inch (682-mm) handlebar of the R100RT.

R100T Dimensions, Weights, and Performance

Overall width	29.37 inches
Saddle height	31.9 inches
Overall length	85.8 inches
Overall height	42.5 inches
Wheelbase	57.7 inches
Weight including oil but without fuel	430 pounds
Weight including oil and fuel	474 pounds
Top speed	121 mph
0–100 mph	12.7 seconds

/7 Engine Specifications 1979–80

Model	Bore (mm)	Stroke (mm)	Capacity (cc)	Compression Ratio	Horsepower DIN
R100T	94	70.6	980	9.5:1	65@6600 rpm
R100S	94	70.6	980	9.5:1	70@7250 rpm

By 1979 all discs featured a new drilled hole pattern, and the fork legs for all markets included reflectors. The silver-anodized ATE brake calipers had 40-mm pistons, evident by the stamp on the exterior.

Also new for 1979 were the handlebar switches. This left side was for U.S. models, without a headlight switch, as the headlight was hard-wired on. The turn-signal switch was now on the left.

1980 R100S, R100T, R100/7, and R80/7

For 1980, reprised the R100S, R100T, R100/7, and R80/7 with only a few updates for the new year. The R80/7 was updated with new carburetor slides and the sidecover decals read "R80" instead of "R80/7." The R100T and R100/7 now featured black rocker covers. BMW made the following changes only to U.S. versions. All U.S. versions (including the R80/7) were given the updates first fitted to U.S. models from August 1979 starting with R100/7 number 6 170 415, and R100S number 6 165 103. The compression ratio for all engines was 8.2:1, and while the 1,000-cc models retained the high 1:2.91 final drive, the R80/7 this year was fitted with a lower 1:3.36 final drive, with

The right handlebar switch from 1979 still was integral with the cam-and-chain throttle assembly.

For the United States, the R100T could be outfitted with a range of options, including a Luftmeister fairing, Krauser panniers, and trunk. U.S. models from 1980 had the air injection emissions system, with a pipe running from the air filter housing to the exhaust port. U.S. models for 1980 also had the new airbox design with flat air filter, but the housing was cast aluminum, rather than the plastic from 1981. The choke cable ran to the handlebar rather than the airbox. *Cycle World*

a W=1.244 speedometer. Again, there was often inconsistency with the actual final drive installed on a particular example, and some R100Ts came with 1:3.20 final drives. The choke lever was moved to the left handlebar, the loud turn-signal beeper was omitted, and they were fitted with the federally mandated 85-mile-per-hour speedometer.

BMW also added two limited editions for the year. One was the limited-edition R100S "Exclusive Sport," in metallic silver with triple-tone blue striping on the fairing, fuel tank, and seat tailpiece. This limited edition also included chrome shock-absorber springs and polished fork legs, rocker covers, and final drive housing. Its rear fender and side covers were silver, with blue "R100S" decals. The cast wheels were also a matching light silver. The second limited edition was a sport version of the R100T, which included a low handlebar and fairing.

With the price continuing to increase (the R100S was $6,595 in 1980), and performance diminishing, it was time for a more serious revision. This appeared in 1981 with the R100CS and R100, while the R80/7 took a turnabout, becoming the highly successful dual-purpose R80 G/S.

/7 Production 1979 and 1980 Model Years

Model	Dates	1978	1979	1980	Total
R60/7 (&T)	09/78–07/80	263			263
R75/7	01/79–07/79		5		5
R80/7 (&N, T)	09/78–07/80	545	2,271	2,278	5,094
R80/7 (United States)	09/78–07/80	103	73	173	349
R100/7	08/78–07/80	393	1,553	1,689	3,635
R100/7 (United States)	09/78–07/80	202	723	419	1,344
R100T	11/78–07/80	58	307	31	396
R100S	09/78–07/80	224	645	1082	1,951
R100S (United States)	09/78–07/80	102	2	48	152
					13,189

1979–80 R45 and R65

The demise of the R60/7 was hastened by the release of a new smaller capacity series, the R45 and R65. These smaller models, introduced for the 1979 model year, incorporated many of the developments that were shared with the larger twins and theoretically paved the way for the future. In many respects, the new twins were functionally superior, and while the R45 wasn't sold in the United States, a concerted attempt was made to promote the R65. However, despite glowing press coverage, the smaller boxers never really endeared themselves to the American psyche. The R65 may have been narrower and more stylish than the big boxers, with better handling, but it remained expensive, underpowered, and relatively heavy.

Central to the new twin was a shorter-stroke engine, known as the type M76* (470 cc) and M84* (650 cc). The shorter stroke allowed shorter cylinders, con-rods, and pistons, with overall engine width reduced by 2.6 inches (66 mm). Both the R45 and R65 had a 9.2:1 compression ratio for 1979, but for 1980 this was reduced to 8.2:1 for U.S. models, further reducing performance.

The crankcases and cylinder heads were essentially the same as for the larger M65* engine, but with a smaller squish area and valves. The R65 had 38-mm inlet and 34-mm exhaust valves, while the R45 had 34- and 32-mm valves.

The updates to the big twins for 1979 were also featured on the smaller engine. These included the single-row cam chain with oil-damped tensioner, O-rings at the base of the cylinders, ignition points in a separate housing, and a dual-sided engine breather setup. Because of the transfer angle with shorter cylinders, the pushrods were inside a hollow cam follower contacting the lower base rather than the top as on the larger twins. The front engine cover differed from that of the larger twins in that the finning was highlighted black.

The smaller twins also featured the spring-loaded driveshaft damper, but had a lighter (6-pound, 6-ounce) flywheel and smaller diameter (160-mm) clutch. The combined weight of the clutch and flywheel was reduced by more than 3 pounds, to 12 pounds, 10 ounces. A low 1:3.44 (9/31) final drive ratio ensured adequate, if underwhelming performance for the R65, while the R45 had an even lower, 1:3.89 ratio.

Although similar to that of the larger twins, and retaining the bolted-on rear subframe, the chassis was simplified, with the frame no longer having oval-section tubing or additional gussets. The swingarm was 2 inches shorter, and there was an improved centerstand.

The Fichtel & Sachs 36-mm center-axle fork had smaller slider boots, cast-in reflectors, and lightweight headlight mounts, and provided much less travel (6.8 inches or 175 mm) than the big-twin fork. The rear shock absorbers also provided less spring travel, at 4.33 inches (110 mm).

Completing the more sporting aspect of the small twins was a 1.85Bx18-inch cast front wheel, with a 3.25x18-inch tire. The rear wheel was a 2.50Bx18-inch with a 4.00x18-inch tire. The front brake was also improved over that of the larger twins, with a double-piston ATE brake caliper for the single-disc front brake. BMW provided a mount for a second disc in the right fork leg, and the master cylinder was moved to the handlebar, improving brake feel over that of the big twins.

The smaller 5.8-gallon angular tank designed by Hans Muth was no longer symmetrical, as the electrics were now mounted on the right side of the central frame tube. There was only one fuel petcock, and further economies extended to the seat, which now incorporated a strap instead of a passenger grab rail. Other features included unique louvered fiberglass sidecovers, larger-diameter instruments (100 mm), a smaller headlight, and twin-bulb taillight. Fuses were moved from the headlight to a plastic housing underneath the right cover. New handlebar switches, also shared with the 1979 R100s, and a single Bosch horn rounded out the equipment.

There was no denying that the R65 was a competent and classy middleweight, but its timing couldn't have been worse for success in the United States. At $3,445, almost half that of the R100RT, it was as expensive as 1,000-cc Japanese motorcycles. By 1980 the price had climbed to $4,230; the power was down, and it needed a revamp.

R45 and R65 Specifications (1979–80)

	R45	R65
Bore (mm)	70	82
Stroke (mm)	61.5	61.5
Capacity (cc)	473	650
Horsepower (DIN)	35 at 7,250 rpm	45@7250 rpm
Compression ratio	9.2:1	9.2:1 (8.2:1)
Carburetors	Bing 64/28/303-304	Bing 64/32/2030-2040
Overall width	27.1 inches	27.1 inches
Overall length	83.1 inches	83.1 inches
Overall height	42.5 inches	42.9 inches
Wheelbase	55.1 inches	55.1 inches
Weight including oil but without fuel	408 pounds	408 pounds
Weight including oil and fuel	452 pounds	452 pounds
Top speed	99 mph	109 mph

The 1979 R100S still presented an imposing profile and was a fine motorcycle. The rectangular chrome mirrors were specifically for Australian versions. This restored example is number 6 070 821.

Replacing the R60/7 for 1979 was the R65, but the smaller boxers were budget models, without the perceived quality of their larger-capacity brothers. Plagued by annoying vibration, the R65 wasn't widely accepted in the United States and was not a great success. *Cycle World*

Chapter 7

100RT and R80RT (1979–84)

When BMW released the full touring R100RT, with the highest price and most equipment in the 1979 lineup, the R100RT supplanted the highly successful R100RS as the flagship of the BMW line. The R100RT was unashamedly aimed at the U.S. market, and at $6,345 was the most expensive production motorcycle available at that time. With its large standard full fairing and excellent detachable Krauser-built saddlebags, the R100RT expanded the capability and was a much better grand touring bike than the sporting RS.

The R100RT established a formula that would ultimately be even more successful, although it began erratically. Initially, the R100RT's reception was lukewarm, particularly in America, and was outsold by the R100RS. Then for 1983, a much cheaper R80RT joined the R100RT, and this model was more successful, eventually resulting in a longer production span than any other post-1969 boxer twin. The final R100RT left the production line at Spandau in 1996, with a total of 57,137 produced.

As it had to compete against the Harley-Davidson FLH-80 Classic in America, with its hard saddlebags, trunk, and tall screen, all for nearly $1,000 less, the R100RT was lavishly equipped. It came standard with an aerodynamically developed fairing based on that of the R100RS, and excellent detachable Krauser-built saddlebags. And a number of detail touches set the R100RT apart from the R100RS.

Ostensibly similar to the R100RS fairing, the R100RT fairing was considerably larger and incorporated air scoops for ventilation. This is from a 1979 road test. *Cycle World*

1979

Although chassis numbers are listed from June to August 1978 in the parts manuals, factory records indicate R100RT production began in September 1978, for the 1979 model year.

The R100RT proved superior over other full-dress touring motorcycles not only in the level of rider protection and comfort, but also in on-the-road performance. The boxer engine was the same 70-horsepower unit of the R100RS (with black rocker covers but without the oil cooler), but as always BMW paid considerable attention to weight reduction. While the Harley FLH-80 Classic weighed in at a massive 722 pounds (328 kilograms) dry, and the Honda Gold Wing 604 pounds (275 kilograms), the claimed dry weight for the R100RT was only 472 pounds (215 kilograms). This emphasis on minimizing weight undoubtedly contributed to the fine road manners of the R100RT, even if U.S. models suffered from overgearing. The standard final drive for Europe was 1:3.0, while the U.S. version received the high 1:2.91 final drive. As with all U.S. 1,000-cc models, there were changes to the carburetor jetting from August 1979, with 165 main and 2.66 needle jets, and a new choke housing on the Bing carburetors. These changes, along with the air intake, new cylinders, pistons, and engine breather appeared from number 6196045, and were intended for the 1980 model year.

Chassis

The basic chassis was shared with the R100RS, and from number 6232420 and U.S. number 6175169, the forks included additional compression spring dampers. The R100RT also expanded the concept of an integral cockpit on a touring motorcycle. Based on the fairing of the R100RS, the R100RT design was also optimized in a wind tunnel to protect the rider from the air stream at all speeds. Even with the higher and wider, 27-inch (690-mm) handlebar fitted to the RT, the frame-mounted, pressure-molded fiberglass fairing offered complete hand protection. Its high windshield was manually adjustable for three rake (over 10 degrees) and height positions. Adjustable through flat spring steel fingers attached to the corners of the screen, this was extremely effective. Air intakes under the turn signals channeled air into the fairing through automotive-style adjustable air vents with a butterfly valve. Carried over from the R100RS fairing was the headlight cover with the same five orange lines, with rectangular parking light above.

The instrument panel was similar to that of the R100RS, with an electronic tachometer, voltmeter, quartz clock, and speedometer. On U.S. models the speedometer was W=1.078, with a W=0.691 for European kilometers-per-hour instruments. There was room on the panel for additional switches and control lamps for the wide range of optional extras. Initially, these included long-distance headlamps and fog lamps, and later flip-out driving lights in place of the air vents. Like the R100RS, the R100RT had a restricted 70 degrees of steering lock due to the panel fitting around the fork tubes. The fork tubes were also sealed in the fairing with rubber boots, and the front of the fairing included the open grill of the pre-1979 R100RS.

The fairing also included two large (6-liter) lockable storage compartments beneath the air vents, but there were some problems with the early-model lids, and these were replaced during 1979. The rearview mirrors mounted on the fairing, and there were new, stronger fairing mounts from number 6165365 and U.S. number 6196836.

Like the R100T, the R100RT came with standard luggage racks for the light (12.5-pound) pair of roomy, lockable saddlebags. As with all the equipment on the R100RT, these bags set the standard for excellence, as they included flush-mounted locks and scissor support braces for the lids. Unfortunately, BMW's new one-key system didn't encompass the saddlebags or their mounts,

R100RT and R80RT Chassis Numbers (1978–84)

Type	Numbers	Model*	Production Dates
R100RT	6115001 to 6117000	1978	06/78–08/78
R100RT	6152001 to 6153000	1979–80	09/78–08/80
R100RT	6155001 to 6160000	1979–80	09/78–08/80
R100RT	6168001 to 6170000	1979–80	09/78–08/80
R100RT	6230001 to 6240000	1981–84	09/80–10/84
R100RT (United States)	6190001 to 6193000	1978	06/78–08/78
R100RT (United States)	6195001 to 6199000	1979–80	09/78–08/80
R100RT (United States)	6240001 to 6241130	1981	09/80–08/81
R100RT (United States)	6241131 to 6242300	1982	09/81–11/82
R100RT (United States)	6242301 to 6243356	1983	08/82–12/83
R100RT (United States)	6243357 to 6245000	1984	07/83–03/84
R80RT	6420001 to 6425000	1983–84	07/82–11/84
R80RT (United States)	6172001 to 6175000	1983	09/82–11/83
R80RT (United States)	6186101 to 6186300	1984	08/83–07/84

*Not model year just model as per official figures

One of the more unusual color combinations for the 1979 R100RT was the metallic brown and Phoenix gold. There was no oil cooler on the RT, and the color of the wheels was a special gold hue. This is a period photo.

R100RT Dimensions, Weights, and Performance (1979–80)

Overall width	29.37 inches
Saddle height	32.3 inches
Overall length	85.8 inches
Overall height	57.7 inches
Wheelbase	57.7 inches
Weight including oil but without fuel	472 pounds
Weight including oil and fuel	516 pounds
Top speed	Approx. 118 mph
0–100 mph	17.8 seconds

The cockpit layout of the 1979 R100RT was similar to that of the R100RS, and included provision for additional switches.

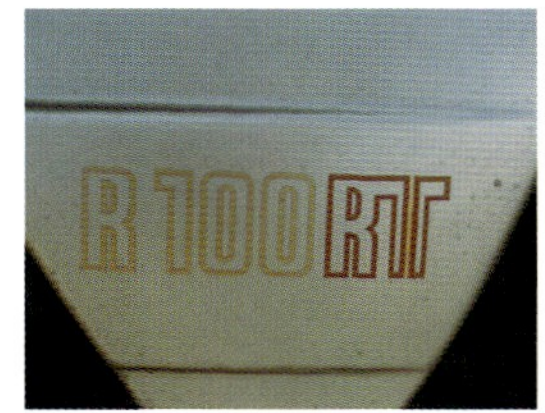

The sidecover decals for 1979 were model specific, and two-tone for the brown-and-gold version.

and two additional keys were required. Standard equipment also included a 12-volt socket behind the left battery panel, a cable lock (with yet another key), and a heel-and-toe rocker gear shift pedal. Shared with the R100RS were the steering damper and twin Fiamm horns.

Other features the R100RT shared with the R100RS included black-painted fork legs, triple disc brakes that were drilled in the new pattern,

Smoke red R100RTs for 1979 had black sidecovers, sometimes without decals as on this example, and silver wheels. With the standard panniers, it beckoned to the open road, but only for the wealthy. This is a period road-test photo. *Cycle World*

One of the options for the R100RT was additional rectangular Hella pop-out driving lights, in place of the air vents. Only a few R100RTs were fitted with these optional lights.

R100RT Production 1979–80 Model Years

Model	Dates	1978	1979	1980	Total
R100RT	08/78-07/80	1,029	3,055	2,270	6,354

twin 40-mm ATE silver-anodized front brake calipers, and a single Brembo rear disc brake. Setting the R100RT apart were cast wheels painted a hue of light gold (Phoenix gold) on the two-tone brown metallic/Phoenix gold metallic version. The other color for 1979 was smoke red, with silver wheels. There was a new seat with strengthened upholstery, and while the upholstery was beige in the publicity brochures, production examples were a more practical black.

1980 R100RT

Along with other U.S. models for 1980, the R100RT received the low-compression pistons (8.2:1), new cylinder heads, the revised air intake and breather system, air induction into the exhaust port, and 38-mm-diameter exhaust pipes, already specified from August 1979 (after number 6 196 045). The engine was still shared with the R100RS, but RTs were not fitted with the oil cooler, and they incorporated the modified lubrication system. The only change to the chassis was new mounts for the wind-wing mirror from December 1979. The price went up yet again, to a then-staggering $7,195.

1981 R100RT

There were many updates for 1981, including a stronger engine housing, shared with the R100CS and R100, and a new sump that enlarged the oil capacity to 2.5 liters, without an oil cooler. There were also the Nikasil barrels, lighter clutch and flywheel, new air filter, electronic ignition, and new final drive casting, as on all R100s this year. With 38-mm exhaust pipes with a second balance pipe, the power remained at 70 horsepower, at a lower 7,000 rpm, for European models. U.S. versions retained the low-compression (8.2:1) pistons and exhaust port air injection (but with a vacuum control).

The frame, wheels (with wider front wheel), front suspension, and Brembo brakes were the same as the R100RS. Some fork legs were plain alloy, although most were still painted black, and from number 6232420 and U.S. number 6175169, the fork included a compression-damping spring.

The main change to the rear suspension was a pair of Boge Nivomat self-leveling shock absorbers. These incorporated a high-pressure oil/gas chamber in the lower part of the body, with a low-pressure chamber in the top. Repeated shock-absorber action saw oil transferred from the top to the lower chamber, with the shock eventually settling at a point determined by the controlling orifice in the central pumping rod. Although the spring travel was reduced to 3.37 inches (85.5 mm), the leveling system was extremely effective, and the Nivomat was the most advanced suspension available for a touring motorcycle in 1981. All wheels were silver, with the special Phoenix gold discontinued.

While the fairing was basically unchanged, the center section was closed off with fewer slots. There was also a new windshield, trimmer than before, and without any creases that distorted the vision, as on the earlier version. The windshield attachment was also improved so allow easier refitting. The range of colors continued to expand, the wide range now including metallic green with gold pinstriping and decals. The R100RTs also retained the steering damper. The price rose slightly, to $7,300.

1982–84 R100RT and R80RT

There were only a few developments to the R100RT for 1982, including a new frame (from January), and new transmission components (from April). The standard panniers were of a new rectangular shape, and from U.S. R100RT number 6242152 there was a new rear turn signal bracket.

Although the price of the R100RT was unchanged for 1982, sales never achieved expectations, particularly in the United States, where it was expected to sell best. In an attempt to address this, in July 1982, BMW offered a considerably cheaper RT, the R80RT. Combining the engine of the R80 G/S with the R100 chassis and R100RT fairing, the R80RT offered a similar touring experience for only $5,490, over $1,500 less than the R100RT. It became available in the United States for 1983. Even though the R80RT didn't include many of the luxury features that distinguished the R100RT, it provided outstanding value, as long as ultimate performance wasn't a consideration. The large frontal area of the RT fairing taxed the mildly tuned engine to the limit, so acceleration and top speed were leisurely.

U.S. and European R80RTs both used the same engine, basically the same as the earlier R80/7, but with the lower 8.2:1 compression ratio, Nikasil cylinders, lighter clutch and flywheel, and electronic ignition. There were new valve seats for the 42- and 38-mm valves, and shorter (44-mm) valve guides. Distinguishing the R80RT were plain alloy, rather than black, rocker covers. To compensate for the moderate horsepower, the R80RT came with a 1:3.36 (37:11) final drive ratio. The speedometer was a W=1.244 for miles per hour and W=0.773 for kilometers per hour. There were new 32-mm Bing carburetors for the R80RT, with different throttle return springs. From May 1983 all R80 carburetors had new

For 1981 the R100RT shared the engine and chassis developments of the other R100s that year. Also new were the rearview mirror mounts.

R80RT Engine Specifications 1983–84

Model	Bore (mm)	Stroke (mm)	Capacity (cc)	Compression Ratio	Horsepower DIN
R80RT	84.8	70.6	797	8.2:1	50@6500 rpm

R80RT Carburetors

	R80RT
Left Carburetor	Bing 64/32/305 (323 U.S.)
Right Carburetor	Bing 64/32/306 (324 U.S.)
Main Jet	150
Needle Jet	2.66
Jet Needle No.	46-241
Needle Position	3
Idle Jet	40

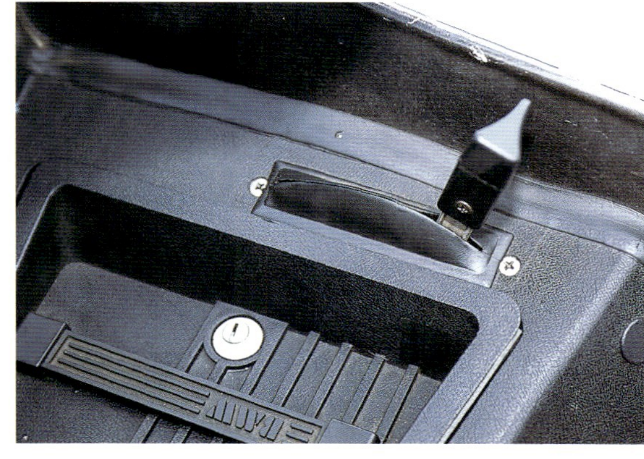

Inside the RT fairing were useful, lockable storage compartments. The lever operates the retractable optional driving lights.

Far right: Automotive-style adjustable fresh-air vents were located inside the R100RT and R80RT fairing on those models without driving lights.

The large fairing and adjustable windshield contributed to a significant frontal area that hurt top-end performance but provided incredible rider protection. This 1981 R100RT (number 623537) is close to original and unrestored. The older style Krauser panniers were fitted this year.

Apart from slightly different instruments and a warning-light console, the cockpit of the 1981–84 R100RT was identical to that of the earlier versions. Also standard was the steering damper, and this example includes a hazard warning flasher next to the steering damper knob.

needles, throttle valves, and 135 main jets, while U.S. versions now had a 40 idling jet and 2.68 atomizer. The Bosch electronic ignition system was the same as for the R100 versions, but with different spark plugs, Bosch W7D, Beru 14-7D, or Champion N10Y.

The R80RT's fairing included an adjustable windshield, but the smaller RT had no voltmeter, clock, or luggage as standard equipment. These were extra cost options. The front fork was also the same as the R100RT's, but with unpainted fork legs. While the front wheel and twin Brembo brakes were from the R100RT, the rear wheel and brake were the 2.50Bx18-inch wheel and rod-operated 200-mm Simplex brake of the R100. The rear suspension was also the standard R100 Boge twin shock absorbers, with the Nivomat self-levelers optional. Standard equipment included the steering damper, twin Fiamm horns, and external power socket. The year 1983 also saw the return of the 140-mile-per-hour speedometer for U.S. versions.

Ironically, just as the 1,000-cc twins were about to be superseded, the R100RT finally became accepted in America. But the success of the R80RT eclipsed even that of the rejuvenated R100RT, and it was the 800-cc version that survived in the wake of the new K series. The R80RT then reappeared in 1985, followed by a new R100RT in 1988.

R100RT and R80RT Dimensions, Weights, and Performance (1981–84)

Model	R100RT	R80RT
Overall width	29.37 inches	29.37 inches
Saddle height	32.3 inches	32.3 inches
Overall length	87.0 inches	87.0 inches
Overall height	57.7 inches	57.7 inches
Wheelbase	57.7 inches	57.7 inches
Weight including oil but without fuel	478 pounds	471 pounds
Weight including oil and fuel	522 pounds	518 pounds
Top speed	Approx. 118 mph	Approx 100 mph
0-400 meters	13.5 seconds	NA

R100RT and R80RT Production 1981–84 Model Years

Model	Dates	1980	1981	1982	1983	1984	Total
R100RT	08/80–10/84	1,140	2,910	2,512	909	45	7,516
R100RT (United States)	09/80—9/84	729	1,292	549	1,284	291	4,145
R80RT	07/82–11/84			1,638	2,539	986	5,163
R80RT (United States)	08/82–10/84			632	967	553	2,152
							18,976

Chapter 8

R80 G/S and R80ST

Following on the success of the R90S and R100RS was another milestone motorcycle, the R80 G/S. The G/S stood for Gelände Strasse, or woods/street, and like its illustrious predecessors, the R80 G/S rewrote the rules, pioneering a new class of motorcycle. This category, an all-purpose large-capacity leisure machine, was immediately successful and initiated a path that serves BMW well today with the R1150GS and Adventurer.

Although now dwarfed by its newer incarnations, when it was released, the R80 G/S was the world's largest dual-purpose motorcycle. Aimed at the explorer or adventurer rider, for a dirt bike the R80 G/S was big and heavy, but for a street motorcycle the weight and size were moderate. Off-road performance was compromised, but as the weight was less than that of the pure street R100 and R80 versions the G/S was an exceptionally capable street machine.

So successful was the R80 G/S during the first two years of production that for 1983 it spawned a pure street version, the R80ST (Street Touring). Although this was expected to expand the street capability of the R80 G/S, the R80ST didn't meet with the same response in the marketplace and was discontinued after two years.

In the meantime the R80 G/S was the only boxer twin to survive the advent of the K series unscathed, and it formed the basis of the final series of "air-head" twins. While the R80 G/S was extremely popular in Europe, in the United States it suffered from a price of $4,800, when Japanese 500-cc single-cylinder dual-purpose bikes sold for less than $2,000. As a result, relatively few were

Although designed as a dual-purpose model, the R80 G/S was one of the most competent BMW street motorcycles. It initiated a line of boxer motorcycles that would become one of the most successful. This is one of the first, a 1981 model (number 6254142) and is unrestored.

The engine of the R80 G/S was similar in specification to the R80/7 engine, but the chassis was a development of the smaller R65.

New for the R80 G/S was a lighter and stronger final drive housing, and a Monolever single-sided swingarm. The shock absorber mounted to the swingarm on the R80 G/S.

sold in the United States during 1981 and 1982, but there has been renewed interest in the R80 G/S in recent years. It now emulates the R90S and R100RS in classic status.

1981–82 R80 G/S

After several years of successful official involvement in the ISDT (International Six Days Trials) and German and European enduro championships with specially prepared enduro boxer twins, BMW's release of the R80 G/S wasn't totally unexpected. During 1980, while the development of the R80 G/S was under way, Werner Schütz won the German championship and Rolf Witthöft the European championship, but the R80 G/S differed considerably from these special racers. The R80 G/S was unique. Using the R80/7 engine and an R65 chassis, it continued on a path of evolutionary development.

R80 G/S and R80ST Chassis Numbers (1981–87)

Type	Numbers	Model Year	Production Dates
R80 G/S	6250001 to 6260000	1981–87	09/80–10/87
R80 G/S	6281001 to 6290000	1981–87	09/80–10/87
R80 G/S	6291001 to 6292600	1981–87	09/80–10/87
R80 G/S (United States)	6362001 to 6362748	1981	09/80–05/81
R80 G/S (United States)	6262766 to 6362883	1983	08/81–09/82
R80 G/S (United States)	6362884 to 6363059	1984	09/83–09/84
R80 G/S (United States)	6363060 to 6363157	1985	01/85–03/85
R80 G/S (United States)	6363158 to 6363350	1986	09/85–12/85
R80ST	6054001 to 6060000	1983–84	11/82–10/84
R80ST (United States)	6207001 to 6207701	1983	10/82–06/83
R80ST (United States)	6207702 to 6207980	1984	08/83–07/84

Engine and Drivetrain

As the R80/7 was discontinued for 1981, the R80 G/S was now the only 800-cc model available. The general engine specifications were similar to the R80/7 engine, and identical to the R80RT engine already described in chapter 7. While the G/S engine's power output remained the same as the R100/7's, the new engine produced slightly less torque at higher rpm (41.8 ft-lb at 5,000 rpm compared to 43.5 ft-lb at 3,500 rpm).

Developments extended to the strengthened crankcases, Nikasil or Galnikal cylinders, breakerless electronic ignition with a microelement voltage regulator, 10-pound-lighter clutch and flywheel, and plastic airbox with flat air filter. Models for California had slightly different crankcases.

The R80 G/S engine included a smaller oil sump than the other 1981 twins, a different dipstick, and a sump protector. Sump capacity was slightly less, at 2.4 quarts (2.25 liters). Also unique to the R80 G/S was its high-rise, two-into-one exhaust system, consisting of twin 38-mm header pipes feeding into a premuffler and a high muffler on the left. The system was painted black.

The clutch and five-speed gearbox were the same as for the 1981 R100, but with a stronger diaphragm spring. The R80 G/S included only the kickstart as standard, with the lower ratio for 1981. The R80 G/S final drive ratio was 1:3.36 (11/37), and these gears were housed in a new pressure die-cast final drive housing.

The G/S's Bing V64 carburetors included an additional throttle slide location for a lighter action, and the choke lever was on the left handlebar. The throttle cable assembly featured a one-into-two junction for improved synchronization, and the rubber sleeve air hose connecting to the air filter box was no longer specific for 32-mm carburetors but the same as for the 40-mm units.

Electrical System and Ignition

The 280-watt alternator, Wehrle E 1051 B/14V voltage regulator, and Bosch TSZH electronic ignition were all shared with the R100. The R80 G/S spark plugs were Bosch W7D, Beru 175/14/3A or 14/7 DU, or Champion N10Y or N9YC. The plug caps were the earlier suppressed type, similar to those of the /6, and the ignition coil was a double-ended Bosch, as fitted to the post-1981 R65 (but not the R100). These gray-cased coils were one of the few unreliable components on the motorcycle. Powering the electrical system was a much smaller 9-Ah battery. An option (standard in the United States) was an electric start with a 0.7-kilowatt Bosch starter motor, and a larger 16-Ah battery. As with the R65, many of the electrical components were located on the right side of the frame's backbone tube.

Frame and Suspension

The frame for the R80 G/S was similar to that of the R65, without an additional strengthening tube in the backbone. The frame downtubes were

R80 G/S and R80ST Engine Specifications

Bore (mm)	Stroke (mm)	Capacity (cc)	Compression Ratio	Power (DIN)
84.8	70.6	797	8.2:1	50@6,500 rpm

R80 G/S and R80ST Carburetors (1981–83)

Left Carburetor	Bing V64/32/305 (321 U.S. models)
Right Carburetor	Bing V64/32/306 (322 U.S. models)
Main Jet	145
Needle Jet	2.64
Jet Needle No.	46-241
Needle Position	4
Idle Jet	45 (40)

The plastic airbox with twin forward-facing snorkel air intakes was shared with all 1981 boxer twins.

As on the R65, many of the R80 G/ S' electrical components were located on the right of the frame backbone tube.

A 21-inch wheel and single front Brembo disc brake was standard on the R80 G/S. This also has an optional steel fork brace.

The 18-inch rear wheel was retained by three automotive-style lug nuts.

The small headlight was incorporated in a plastic housing that also supported the instruments, and the gas tank only had a left-side petcock. White was the only color for 1981, and the handlebar was originally black chrome.

One of the more unusual features of the R80 G/S was the backward-pivoting gearshift linkage. This was also featured on the R80ST, and later R100GS.

The footpegs and rear brake lever indicated the R80 G/S was an off-road motorcycle, but it was still more suitable for street use.

a sturdy 1.25 inches in diameter, while the bolted-on rear subframe was new, as was the special single-sided swingarm, or Monolever. Also incorporating the driveshaft, the Monolever was claimed to provide 50 percent greater torsional rigidity, while weighing 4.4 pounds (2 kilograms) less than the normal double-sided type. It was also supported in tapered roller bearings. Oil was enclosed inside the swingarm, lubricating the driveshaft.

The G/S used a 36-mm front fork that was similar in internal design to that of the R65, but the G/S fork was a leading axle type with provision for dual-disc brakes. The fork legs included cast-in reflector mounts. Fork travel was the same 7.9 inches (200 mm) as on the larger twins. Fourteen-rib gaiters protected the fork tubes, and the top triple clamp was specific for the R80 G/S (and R80ST). The rear suspension was by a single Boge shock absorber, providing 6.69 inches (170 mm) of travel. As this attached at the junction of the main frame and rear subframe, the entire structure was more rigid than that of the twin-shock examples.

Wheels, Tires, and Brakes

A front 1.85Bx21-inch hardened alloy wheel rim was laced to the cast-alloy hub with 40x4-mm straight pull spokes, while at the rear was a 2.15Bx18-inch rim. The rim profile was designed to facilitate quick tire changes. The Metzeler Enduro tires were specifically developed for the R80 G/S, a 3.00x21-inch for the front and 4.00x18-inch on the rear. These were the first universal tires to be rated at speeds up to 106 miles per hour. The rear wheel was retained automotive style by three 12-mm nuts.

The R80 G/S had a single 260-mm front disc brake with a 38-mm twin-piston Brembo caliper (as fitted to the R65). The 13-mm master cylinder was integral to the Magura throttle assembly. Starting in September 1981, BMW began fitting a new front master cylinder with a 12-mm piston. Asbestos-free, semimetallic brake pads were also a new development. The rear brake was the usual rod-operated 200-mm Simplex drum.

Fuel Tank, Side Panels, and Fenders

The fuel tank was similar in shape to that of the R65, and constructed to allow for the electrical components on the right side of the frame backbone tube. It also included only one petcock (on the left), but was slightly smaller at 5.1 gallons (19.5 liters). The filler cap incorporated a ventilation tube, and was therefore nonlockable. California versions had a complicated venting system between the fuel tank and air box. The high front fender, black rear fender, and sidecovers were plastic. The color for 1981 was white, with blue and purple decorative tank panels.

Seat and Frame Fittings

BMW gave the G/S a unique red/orange or blue seat that was 23.6 inches (600 mm) long, with a plastic base. It was lockable, but could be removed. A passenger grab rail was incorporated in the rear subframe. There was only one storage compartment under the seat, with the usual complete toolkit and tire pump (fitting into the backbone tube). A first-aid kit wasn't included as there was no room inside the seat padding. The R80 G/S featured a high and wide 32-inch (820-mm) enduro-style black-chrome handlebar with a strengthening brace, and round matte black rearview mirrors. The fork lock on early G/Ss required a separate key from the ignition and seat, but later G/Ss were equipped with the one-key locking system.

The footpegs, gear shift lever, and rear brake pedal were all specifically designed for the R80 G/S. The nonadjustable footpegs were a folding motocross type with saw-toothed tips and strong return springs. The gear shift lever was stamped steel, unusually pivoting backward on the frame, and connecting to the transmission with a rod and ball joint. Only a centerstand was fitted, this receiving a stronger return spring and new spring bracket after October 1981. Black engine protection bars with integral sidestand were optional. The sidestand, as with all for 1981, was not self-retracting. Other options included a windshield, pannier (on the right side only), and luggage rack.

Electrics, Controls, Instruments, Headlight, and Taillight

Most of the controls were standard 1981 BMW fare, including the handlebar switches, Magura levers, and rectangular turn-signals with black plastic bodies. Instead of the Fiamm horns, there was a single, round black Bosch horn similar to that of the /6. The black plastic instrument housing contained a speedometer (85 miles per hour for the United States in 1981), with a W=1.244 drive or W=0.773 (kilometers per hour) drive. The miles-per-hour speedometer also indicated kilometers per hour and included was a push-button trip-odometer reset. A tachometer and quartz clock were optional.

The array of warning lights included turn, high beam, generator, oil, and neutral, with the ignition key located under the generator light. There were no turn-signal beepers but for some reason, both the neutral and turn signal warning lights were green. The instrument pod incorporated the 5.5-inch (140-mm) Bosch H4 headlight. The taillight was a single chamber type, with one 21/5-watt bulb.

There were few changes to the R80 G/S for 1982. The electric start was now standard, and the rear wheel rim was increased to a 2.50Bx18-inch. A blue version (with red and blue decorative tank panels) with a black seat was also available. One key locking was standard, and from number 627262, and U.S. number 6362765, BMW began fitting a new frame. The optional right-side pannier was the new rectangular type. The price dropped to $4,100 for 1982.

The only instrument fitted to the R80 G/S was a MotoMeter speedometer.

This single-bulb taillight was specific to the R80 G/S.

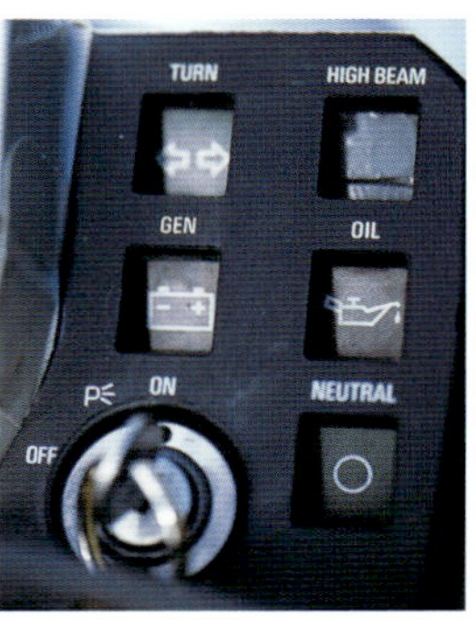

Flanking the speedometer on the right was this panel of warning lights.

R80 G/S Dimensions, Weights, and Performance

Overall width	29.37 inches
Saddle height	33.9 inches
Overall length	87.8 inches
Overall height	45.3 inches
Wheelbase	57.7 inches
Weight including oil but without fuel	368 pounds (381 pounds with electric start)
Weight including oil and fuel	410 pounds (423 pounds with electric start)
Top speed	104 mph
0-400 meters (1,312 feet)	13.8 seconds

R80 G/S and R80ST Carburetors (from May 1983)

Left Carburetor	Bing 64/32/349 (351 U.S. models)
Right Carburetor	Bing 64/32/350 (352 U.S. models)
Main Jet	135 (132)
Needle Jet	2.68 (2.66)
Jet Needle No.	46-251
Needle Position	3 (2)
Idle Jet	45

1983–84 R80 G/S and R80ST

Joining the R80 G/S for 1983 was a pure street-only version, the R80ST. This was very similar to the R80 G/S, with the same engine and Monolever chassis, but with a few street accouterments.

There were only detail differences in the engine department between the two models. The R80ST had the same deeper sump as R100 twins from 1981, with no protective plate, along with a different intake for the oil pump (the same as the R80RT). The R80 G/S oil pump intake was from the R80/7. A kickstart was not standard on the R80ST, and the rocker covers were black, rather

Joining the successful R80 G/S for 1983 was a street version, the R80ST, but it didn't meet with much acclaim. Like all U.S. models, this example features exhaust port air injection, and rear side reflectors. Red models included white pinstripes. This is from a period road test. *Cycle World*

There was a smaller, 19-inch front wheel for the R80ST, but the single front disc brake remained. The fork front was a center-axle type, but the fork gaiters on this example weren't standard. This is an unrestored silver-gray 1984 model.

than plain aluminum. The two-into-one exhaust system was similar to that of the R80 G/S, but it was chrome-plated and incorporated an insulated black cover plate. This enabled the optional panniers to be fitted on both sides instead of the right side only.

The R80ST was also the first model to feature the revised gear shift cam plate, but this soon was fitted to the entire range. The final drive ratio was the same as for the R80 G/S, with a higher 1:3.20 (10:32) an option. Developments during the year (on both the R80ST and R80 G/S), from May 1983, included new throttle slides and slide needles for the Bing carburetors, a larger O-ring at the slide base, and a new top housing for the air filter. The carburetors were a new type V 64 II. As starting was electric only, the R80ST included the larger 16-Ah battery of the electric start R80 G/S.

While the frame and Monolever swingarm of the R80ST was shared with the R80 G/S, there was a different front fork and rear shock. Although some early brochures displayed the R80ST with the R80 G/S leading axle front fork, all production examples featured an R65-style center axle fork. The fork legs were unpainted alloy, with integral cast reflectors, with a provision for dual front disc brakes. The fork tubes were longer than those of the R65, and included a lower compression spring (like the larger twins). The fork travel was 6.9 inches (175 mm). At the rear was a shortened R80 G/S Boge shock absorber providing slightly less travel (6.0 inches, or 153 mm).

Also different for the R80ST was a wire-spoked 1.85Bx19-inch front wheel. At the rear was the same 2.50Bx18-inch rear wheel as on the G/S. Tires were street pattern, in sizes of 100/90H19 and 120/90H18. Also shared with the R80 G/S was the single Brembo front disc, and 200-mm rear Simplex drum brake. From March 1983, BMW began fitting a new cover for the rear brake housing on both the R80ST and R80 G/S. From September 1983 the R80 G/S had a new gas-charged shock absorber with a remote reservoir, along with a new rear brake lever.

Most of the bodywork of the R80ST was similar to that of the R80 G/S. The fuel tank was slightly smaller (20.14 quarts or 19 liters), with a

R80ST Dimensions, Weights, and Performance

Overall width	29.37 inches
Saddle height	33.3 inches
Overall length	85.8 inches
Overall height	45.3 inches
Wheelbase	57.7 inches
Weight including oil but without fuel	403.5 pounds
Weight including oil and fuel	437 pounds
Top speed	108 mph

The R80ST engine included the deeper sump of the 1981 R100, while the more rigid Monolever contributed to improved handling over the twin-shock models. The exhaust system included a premuffler under the transmission. Silver-gray examples had red pinstriping.

single petcock, and it included a lockable filler cap. The front and rear plastic fenders were color-matched, along with more extensive side panels, particularly on the left to cover the high muffler. Two colors were offered, metallic red or metallic silver-gray.

Where the R80ST departed from the R80 G/S most significantly was in the instrument panel. BMW gave the ST the panel from the R65, which included a larger 3.9-inch (100-mm) speedometer and tachometer, with a central ignition and headlight switch. The speedometer was a W=0.773 for kilometers per hour, or W=1.244 for miles per hour. Its electronic tachometer included generator, oil, neutral, and high-beam warning lights. The 6.3-inch (160-mm) Bosch H4 headlight (also from the R65), was supported by a special bracket that attached to the top of the fork legs under the top triple clamp.

Apart from the chrome-plated 26.52-inch (680-mm) handlebar (shared with the U.S. R65), all the handlebar controls were the same as on the R80 G/S and the R100 models. Standard on the R80ST were chrome-plated engine-protection bars, with an integral sidestand with dual springs.

Although on paper the R80ST looked to have all the credentials of the perfect street motorcycle, the reality was that it was a parts-bin special. The high-rise exhaust system looked incongruous, and its performance was only moderate for the price of $4,190 ($4,300 in 1984). As a result only 980 R80STs were sold in the United States. The model was discontinued at the end of model year 1984.

The larger-diameter speedometer and tachometer, along with the panel and handlebar padding, came from the R65. Optional accessories included the clock and voltmeter.

The handlebar-mounted front master cylinder with rectangular fluid reservoir was used on all models from 1981.

Also standard throughout the lineup from 1981 was the clutch and choke lever assembly on the left handlebar.

There were specific footpeg rubbers for the R80ST, and the footpegs pivoted.

Although the engine performance was only adequate, the R80ST was one of the lightest and best handling boxer twins. Factory panniers could also be fitted on both sides rather than only on the right, as with the R80 G/S. In many ways it is an underrated motorcycle and deserves more recognition.

1984 R80 G/S Paris-Dakar

Responding to its success in the Paris-Dakar rallies of 1981, 1983, and 1984, BMW released a special Paris-Dakar version of the R80 G/S during 1984. The Paris-Dakar was created by topping the R80 G/S with a few special parts. While the engine and chassis were unchanged, setting the Paris-Dakar apart most notably was a large steel (8.3-gallon or 32-liter) fuel tank painted white and carrying Paris-Dakar rally winner Gaston Rahier's signature. Also added were red and blue Motorsport decals, foam kneepads, and a red solo seat with fixed black-painted luggage rack and enough capacity to allow for 300 miles between stops. The fenders were white plastic, with a different rear fender than that of the regular G/S, and plastic sidecovers were omitted. Access under the seat required removal of the rack, which was rather inconvenient. While the exhaust header pipes were still black, the Paris-Dakar was fitted with a stainless-steel muffler with a black cover. The battery was a larger, 20-Ah unit. Black engine protection bars and sidestand were standard. All these extras pumped up the weight to 451 pounds (205 kilograms).

1985–87 R80 G/S

In 1984 a team of factory R80 G/Ss was triumphant in the Baja 1,000 off-road race, winning the Class-30 competition, and this led to heightened interest in the R80 G/S in America for 1985. BMW was ready, with many updates to the G/S, which had been essentially unchanged from 1981–84. For 1985, BMW fitted the G/S, the R80 G/S, and Paris-Dakar with an updated engine shared with the rest of the rejuvenated R80 series. BMW began fitting new cylinder heads, with revised bases and supports for the rocker shafts. To eliminate noise emanating from the valve operating mechanism, from January 1985 there were new rockers with axial bearings and plastic washers. Axial end float was now 0.03–0.07 mm (instead of nil). Further noise reduction came through the installation of rubber buttons between the cylinder head fins. The valve seat material was also changed to overcome the valve seat recession problem with unleaded fuel. Starting in February 1985 BMW began fitting a new crankcase oil-pressure relief valve with a 16-mm (instead of 11-mm) compression spring, and a 14-mm blind plug.

Further development occurred in March 1985, with a new input shaft, kickstart spline, input helical driving gear, and thrust mount. The final drive assembly and casting for the 1985 model year was also new, although the ratios were unchanged. This included a new crown wheel set, and a 25x47x15-mm inner tapered roller bearing (from the K series) instead of the previous 35x50x20-mm needle-roller type.

There were also new carburetors for U.S. models for the 1985 model year, Bing 64/32/357-358, with smaller 130 main jets and new diaphragm springs. Starting in September 1984, the throttle and cover were revised. Beginning with the 1985 model year, all versions had the larger 20-Ah battery. BMW continued selling the R80 G/S and Paris-Dakar for 1986 with no change, but for 1987 the company offered it in

A red solo seat and small luggage rack also distinguished the Paris-Dakar R80 G/S. Rather than an out-and-out dirt bike, this was a machine designed for exploring the outback, and it was without peer in this environment.

New for 1984 was a Paris-Dakar R80 G/S. Created to commemorate BMW's victories in the Paris-Dakar desert race during the early 1980s, this was a cosmetic variation on the successful R80 G/S.

new colors. One featured a red fuel tank, with new red sidecover decals, while the other included a blue tank (and seat), with blue decals. The seat shape was slightly different, while the headlight surround was white this year, and there were black rocker covers. A Paris-Dakar shielded muffler on all G/Ss also allowed for the fitting of a left-side pannier.

1988 R65GS

For 1988, the Paralever R80GS (without the "slash") replaced the R80 G/S. Nevertheless, the earlier R80 G/S lived on as a new model—the R65GS—combining the old Monolever chassis with the 650-cc, 82x61.5-mm engine from the R65. It was sold only in the German market. With an 8.4:1 compression ratio and Bing 64/26/317-8 26-mm carburetors, the R65GS engine produced 27 horsepower at 5,500 rpm. The white R65GS looked visually identical to the 1987 R80 G/S, but even in Germany, it proved unpopular. It was built for the 1988–92 model years. Far more successful was the new R100GS, destined to become another classic.

Each Paris-Dakar 8.3-gallon (31.45-liter) gas tank came with a Gaston Rahier signature, BMW Motorsport colors, and rubber kneepads.

R80 G/S, R80ST, R65GS
Production 1981–92

Model	Build Dates	Total
R80 G/S	1980–87	21,864
R80ST	1982–84	5,963
R65GS	1987–92	1,727

Chapter 9

R100CS and R100 (1981–84)

With its wire-spoked wheels and small handlebar fairing, the R100CS recollected the days of the R90S, but provided superior brakes and handling. Although some 1981 brochures showed the R100CS with wire-spoked wheels, generally they were only available for the Australian market. This is an Australian 1982 example.

A rationalization of the lineup coincided with the introduction of the improved A10 engine for 1981. BMW cut its basic R100 line to two. While the R100S continued as the R100CS, there was now only one basic model in the range, the R100. Although still offered for police applications as the R80TIC, the only regular 800-cc model this year was the R80 G/S. However, its outstanding success led to a proliferation of 800-cc versions during 1982 and 1983.

1981 R100CS and R100

Descended from the R90S, the R100CS may have appeared outdated, but it was the strongest performing model in the lineup. BMW powered it with the new A10 engine. Model rationalization saw the R100CS share the new A10 engine of the R100RT. This included the strengthened engine housing, larger sump with 2.5-liter capacity, 38-mm header pipes (with second balance pipe), new air box, lighter clutch, electronic ignition, and new final drive casting. While European R100CSs featured 9.5:1 pistons, all U.S. engines were 8.2:1, with exhaust port air injection. The A10 engine put out 70 horsepower, 3 more than the standard R100 engine. Setting the R100CS apart from the R100 were the black rocker covers. With the best power-to-weight ratio in the BMW stable, the R100CS was considered the sprint model, but was still more than capable as an effortless high-speed tourer.

All R100s were fitted with the 8.2:1-compression pistons, and all featured Bing 94 model 40-mm carburetors. All U.S. R100s retained the 1:2.91 final drive, with the European R100 featuring the 1:3.0 ratio. As before, a wide range of optional equipment was available for the R100, including engine protection bars, Nivomat shock absorbers, electrically heated handlebar grips, white or black panniers, magnetic tank bag, additional instruments, and a super toolkit. The optional touring windshield for the R100 was redesigned, with simplified mounts.

While some brochures and catalogs showed wire-spoked wheels and plain alloy fork legs on the R100CS, most examples had black fork legs and cast wheels. Only a few R100CSs were sold in the United States, and all these had cast wheels. Unlike the preceding R100S, which had a rear disc brake, the R100CS had the narrower 2.50Bx18-inch rear wheel with a rear drum brake. This rear wheel, with new brake lever, brake shoes, and brake cam, was also shared with the R100. Both the R100CS and R100 front cast wheels were wider than previous R100 wheels, at 2.15Bx19-inch, and all included the double Brembo disc brakes with metallic pads. There were no black fork legs for the base R100, and from number 6193063, the front fork included additional compression springs.

The R100CSs with wire-spoked wheels (mainly for the Australian market) had different hubs to the earlier types, with new distance bushings. The alloy rim sizes were the same as on the R100S of 1977, a 1.85Bx19-inch on the front and a 2.15Bx18-inch on the rear with a 200-mm Simplex rear brake.

Many R100CSs were painted black, with gold pinstriping, and the most popular color for the R100 was silver with blue pinstripes.

The R100CS had specific "R100CS" sidecover decals this year, and all R100s included the new front fender brace. There were new, black, round mirrors for both the R100CS and R100, with the frame tube cable lock still featured on the R100CS (optional on the R100). The ignition lock was on the left headlight mount, and the front master cylinder was integral with the Magura twistgrip. While twin Fiamm horns graced the R100CS, the R100 still only had a single horn on the left. However, at only $5,350 it offered arguably the best value in the R100 lineup. The asking price of the R100CS was $6,600.

1982–84 R100CS and R100

The R100CS was dropped from the U.S. lineup for 1982 and 1983, although a few trickled in through 1984. Instead of the R100CS and R100, BMW offered two versions of the R100 for the

R100CS and R100 Chassis Numbers (1981–84)

Type	Numbers	Model Year	Production Dates
R100CS	6135001 to 6140000	1981–84	09/80–10/84
R100CS (United States)	6188001 to 6188163	1981	09/80–03/81
R100CS (United States)	6188164 to 6188170	1982–83	
R100CS (United States)	6188171 to 6188174	1984	
R100	6035001 to 6040000	1981–84	09/80–11/84
R100	6400001 to 6405000	1981–84	09/80–11/84
R100 (United States)	6175001 to 6175593	1981	09/80–03/81
R100 (United States)	6175594 to 6176221	1982	09/81–06/82
R100 (United States)	6176222 to 6176785	1983	08/82–12/83
R100 (United States)	6176789 to 6178000	1984	06/83–03/84
R100 (United States)	6186001 to 6186100	1984	04/84–10/84

R100CS and R100 Engine Specifications

Model	Bore (mm)	Stroke (mm)	Capacity (cc)	Compression Ratio	Horsepower DIN
R100CS R100	94	70.6	980	9.5:1	70@7000 rpm
R100CS US	94	70.6	980	8.2:1	67@7000 rpm

The R100CS had the higher specification R100RS/RT engine, and black rocker covers. All R100 engines from 1981 had the deeper sump and plastic airbox, and this one also has an optional kickstart.

A new, never used 1981 R100. This had a lower-compression motor, but still came with 40-mm carburetors. Unlike the R100RS and RT, the R100 had a rear drum brake and a slightly narrower rear wheel rim. Right: The 1981 R100 also included a remote gear shift linkage with a protective rubber bellows. There was no grease nipple for the pivot.

U.S., the Touring and the Sport, both listed at $5,350. These were U.S. designations and not differentiated in production figures. The Sport came standard with the CS sport fairing and narrow handlebar, while the Touring was fitted with standard saddlebags. As so few R100CSs were sold in the United States, this seemed a prudent move to standardize specifications, and there was no doubt that the new Sport was a much better value than the CS. Both R100s included nonpainted fork legs and black rocker covers, "R100" sidecover decals, and cast-alloy wheels with a rear drum brake. During 1982, U.S. versions (from R100CS 6188165 and R100 6175996) also included new rear turn-signal

The R100CS cockpit. Apart from the different switches, handlebar-mounted front master cylinder, and handlebar padding, this could almost be the cockpit of a 1974 R90S. The steering damper was an option.

R100CS and R100 Dimensions, Weights and Performance (1981–84)

Model	R100CS	R100
Overall width	29.37 inches	29.37 inches
Saddle height	32.3 inches	32.3 inches
Overall length	87.0 inches	87.0 inches
Overall height	47.6 inches	42.5 inches
Wheelbase	57.7 inches	57.7 inches
Weight including oil but without fuel	441 pounds	437 pounds
Weight including oil and fuel	485 pounds	481 pounds
Top speed	Approx. 118 mph	106 mph
0-400 meters	13.5 seconds	

brackets. From April 1982 there were new transmission components (input and fifth gears). For 1983, prices were reduced to $4,990 for the R100 Touring and $5,190 for the R100 Sport.

For Europe the R100CS and R100 were still offered during 1982 and 1983, with black fork legs and cast-alloy wheels. They continued for 1984 with plain fork legs, and "R100" sidecover decals. There was also an extremely rare R100CS Motorsport, dark blue with orange and light blue pinstripes.

The R100CS was also listed for the United States for 1984 (at $5,500), but few were available. The price of the R100 (Sport and Touring) increased marginally to $5,300 for 1984, and just as production was about to end, it sold more strongly in the United States than in the rest of the world.

1981–84 R45, R65, and R65LS

The developments to the larger twins also trickled through to the smaller R45 and R65 for 1981, with the new engine type designated the A20. In an effort to restore the power to 1979 levels, inside the cylinder head were larger (40- and 36-mm) valves. As with the R100, there were Nikasil cylinders, the clutch and flywheel were lighter, and the ignition was electronic. O-ring grooves were now machined in the base of the cylinders. There was also an additional cross-over pipe in the exhaust, extra cushioning in the driveshaft, and a larger sump, increasing oil capacity. Only the R65 was sold in the United States, and these featured the revised air-injection system of the larger twins with vacuum shut-off inside the plastic air box. European versions had a 9.2:1 compression ratio, while U.S. examples retained the 8.2:1 pistons. There were two versions of the R45, a higher-compression 35-horsepower model with 28-mm carburetors, and a particularly strangulated 27-horsepower version (with 26-mm carburetors) for Germany's special insurance category.

The general chassis layout was unchanged, although there were some subtle changes to the steering geometry, to 3.78 inches (96 mm) of trail. U.S. models were fitted with dual-disc front brakes as standard, with a 16-mm master cylinder. The swingarm was stronger, 10 mm longer, and constructed of larger-diameter tubing with additional gusseting. The new final drive housing was pressure diecast. The new seat incorporated softer foam and thinner padding to lower the seat height to 31.9 inches (810 mm). The 1981 R65 looked virtually identical to the previous version but was an improved machine, and came at a lower price of $3,995.

R100CS and R100 Production 1981–84 Model Years

Model	Dates	1980	1981	1982	1983	1984	Total
R100CS	09/80-10/84	516	1,530	1,276	493	49	3,864
R100CS (United States)	09/80–9/84	126	38	4	3	3	174
R100	09/80-11/84	948	2,666	2,394	594	193	6,795
R100 (United States)	09/80-10/84	358	556	598	673	237	2,422
R100 TIC (Police)	10/80-10/84	9	235	214	284	152	894
							14,149

There was no steering damper on the R100, but a BMW emblem on the handlebar pad took its place. The speedometer reading indicates this 1981 R100 is unused. From 1981 the warning light console included a high-beam light.

The dual-chamber taillight used in 1981 was the same as the 1979 model.

All twins from 1981 had the choke on the left handlebar. This R100 has a hard-wired headlight and no light switch, as featured on U.S. examples.

For 1982 the R65 was joined by the R65LS, with dramatic Hans Muth styling. Underneath the bodywork was an R65 engine and frame, but the R65LS featured a number of unique styling touches. The fork-mounted spoiler incorporated the instrument nacelle, and was claimed to reduce front-end lift by 30 percent. Complementing the nosepiece was a redesigned seat with molded passenger grab rails and a sporting fiberglass front fender. The new seat featured a larger storage box of .115 cubic feet (compared to .08 cubic feet). Two colors were offered, red and silver. The black chrome handlebars were lower, providing a more sporting riding position. The exhaust system was plasma-sprayed in flat black. Unfortunately, this finish was particularly prone to rust.

One of the more distinctive features of the R65LS was the wheels. Still 18-inch front and rear, the front rim was a wider, 2.15-inch, but the

The fork legs were generally black on the R100CS, but not on this example with an R100 chassis. The wire-spoked wheels were fitted to Australian examples in response to public demand, but only a few were sold. This 1982 bike is original and unrestored, and now rare and unusual.

This 1982 R100CS features R100 decals and emblems rather than those of the R100CS, although the specification is R100CS. The frame number (6400013) is also from the R100 series, so it is technically an R100 Sport that was offered alongside the R100 Touring in 1982. Some 1982 twins had fuel petcocks with rear-facing outlets but not this R100.

design was new. Jointly developed by BMW and Alusuisse, the cast-aluminum rim was heat treated for hardening and featured a pressure-cast star-shaped hub. The spokes were curved to provide some elasticity, and this composite setup provided the advantages of both the elasticity of wire-spoked wheels with the rigidity of cast wheels. These wheels were also lighter than the snowflake wheels, .75 kilogram for the front and 1.35 kilograms for the rear. The rear wheel also included a slightly larger, 8.7-inch (220-mm) rod-operated Simplex rear brake. On the R65LS, the wheels were silver on silver-painted LSs and white on red-painted LSs. These new wheels eventually featured on the post-1984 boxer twins.

Early 1982 R65s (including the R65LS) as featured in publicity brochures, were fitted with dual-piston silver-anodized ATE front brake calipers, but most production versions came with black Brembo calipers. Calipers on R65s were the

With its low handlebar, the R65LS replicated the café racer style initiated by the R90S. However, the conservative BMW buyer considered the styling too radical. Although 6,389 R65LSs were produced, very few of this unloved model seem to have survived unscathed.

smaller, 36-mm units, instead of the 38-mm calipers fitted to the R100 twins. While the R65LS came standard with dual front discs, the hydraulic ratio was improved with a smaller (15-mm) master cylinder.

The standard R65 for 1982 featured only a single front disc brake. The price was reduced to $3,600, while the R65LS sold for $3,995. The R65LS went down to $3,900 for 1983, but increased to $4,100 for 1984. As the more practical R80 G/S and R80ST were only $200 more expensive, the R65LS was another short-lived model, not surviving after the end of the 1985 model year. Production of the R45 and R65 also continued until 1985, but they weren't sold in the United States.

R45, R65, and R65LS Specifications (1981–84)

	R45	R65	R65LS
Bore (mm)	70	82	82
Stroke (mm)	61.5	61.5	61.5
Capacity (cc)	473	650	650
Horsepower (DIN)	35 (27) at 7,250 rpm	50 at 7,250 rpm	50@7250 rpm
Compression ratio	9.2:1 (8.2:1)	9.2:1 (8.2:1)	9.2:1 (8.2:1)
Carburetors	Bing 64/28/303-304 (64/26/303-304)	Bing 64/32/307-308	Bing 64/32/307-308
Overall width	27.1 inches	27.1 inches	27.1 inches
Saddle height	31.9 inches	31.9 inches	31.9 inches
Overall length	83.1 inches	83.1 inches	83.1 inches
Overall height	42.5 inches	42.5 inches	42.9 inches
Wheelbase	55.1 inches	55.1 inches	55.1 inches
Weight including oil but without fuel	408 pounds	408 pounds	408 pounds
Weight including oil and fuel	452 pounds	452 pounds	452 pounds
Top speed	99 mph	109 mph	109 mph

Chapter 10

Post-1984 Air-Cooled Twins

Although the new generation water-cooled K series replaced the 1,000-cc twins at the end of model year 1984, the flat twin remained in the lineup in 650- and 800-cc guises. Initially it seemed the revamped twins were only produced to satisfy the traditional enthusiast and to maintain a classic tradition within the company. The successful R80 G/S continued virtually unchanged, but there was limited development to the R80, R80RT, and R65. It was soon evident that the K series three- and four-cylinders weren't as successful as BMW had anticipated, and the R80 series was expanded. As interest in the K series waned, there was renewed appreciation of the older "air-head" boxer twins. By 1988 a complete new lineup of R80-based "air-head" twins, headed by the resurrected R100RS and R100RT, and the Paralever R100GS, joined the K100 and K75. The R100RS and R100RT may have appealed to the traditionalist, but it was the dual-purpose R100GS that sustained the life of the "air-head" twin until the advent of the R259 "oil-head" boxer.

The most successful of the resurrected air-cooled boxers was the GS, including this 1991 R100GS Paris-Dakar. Continuing the success of the R80 G/S, such a large motorcycle may have appeared incongruous as a dual-purpose machine, but it found a niche following.

1985–95 R80, R80RT, and R65

While the K100 represented a radical departure for BMW motorcycles from the time-honored concept initiated with the R32, the R80 and new model R65 (based on the larger R80 and no longer a special smaller model) veered back toward those

roots. In the style of the /5 of 1969, these revamped twins were the antithesis of most mid-1980s motorcycles. Instead of emphasizing engine performance through increased complexity without any consideration to weight savings, the new boxer twins reiterated the traditional formula. Simplicity, agility, and lightness were placed ahead of ultimate size and horsepower. Looking remarkably similar to the pre-1984 twins, the new R80 and R65 offered improved brakes and handling, but were no match in performance to the earlier R100.

For Europe, the R80, and R80RT were produced through 1995, with the R65 finishing in 1993. As there was still unsold stock of the previous 1984 model R65 in the United States, only the R80 models were available for 1985. The R65 was added to the U.S. lineup in 1986. The R80, R80RT, and new model R65 were subsequently available in the United States through 1987. However, only a handful were sold (1,120 R80s and 1,452 R80RTs), as they were still overpriced. The R80 cost $4,300 in 1985 and the R80RT $5,700, and they didn't offer enough perceived value for the money. By 1987 this had climbed to $4,800 for the R80 and $6,250 for the R80RT. It wasn't surprising that only three of each were shipped to the United States during 1987.

Engine and Drivetrain

The 800-cc engine was basically that of the R80ST, but there were a few updates aimed at reducing noise. Twelve silicon-rubber plugs were fitted between the cooling fins, and a revised rocker arm assembly with tight-fitting spacers between rocker arms and support brackets further quieted engine noise. These modifications also appeared on the R80 G/S, as described in chapter 8. There was little change to the general engine specifications from the R80ST. Valve sizes were 42 and 38 mm for the R80 engine and 38 and 34 mm on the R65 engine. Starting in June 1987, the valve seat angles were changed to 43 degrees for the inlet and 30 degrees for the exhaust (from 45 degrees for both) to improve their life on unleaded fuel.

The electronic ignition was still Bosch TSZH, but with the unreliable Bosch double-ended ignition coil of the R80 G/S. Also part of the powerplant package were Bing V64/32/353-354 carburetors (V64/32/359-360 for the R65), a Bosch 280-watt alternator, and a 20-Ah battery. The 32-mm Bing carburetors now shared the larger float bowls of the 40-mm variety. U.S. models retained the air-injection system, and this became an option on European versions from 1991. While the R80 had black rocker covers, the R65 retained plain aluminum covers.

Although it was an improvement over the earlier R80/7 in most respects, the R80 was perceived as expensive and underpowered, compared to most motorcycles in 1985. There were no more R80s for the United States after 1987, but it was sold in Europe nearly a decade longer. This is a 1995 example, and it looks very similar to the R80/7 of 1978.

Alongside the R80 for 1985 was the R80RT. Apart from the Monolever chassis and more complete instrumentation and equipment, this was very similar to the 1984 R80RT. The large fairing taxed the mildly tuned 800-cc engine to the limit, so performance was leisurely. *Cycle World*

One of the improvements for the new R80 was the K-series wheels, and new final drive casting. The shock absorber attached to the final drive rather than to the Monolever swingarm (as on the R80 G/S).

All post-1984 twins had a rear drum brake, and the R80 rear wheel was retained by four lug nuts instead of the three of the R80 G/S wheel.

R80, R80RT, and R65 Engine Specifications (1985–95)

Model	Bore	Stroke	Capacity	Com-pression	Horse-power
(mm)	(mm)	(cc)	Ratio	DIN	
R80/R80RT	84.8	70.6	798	8.2:1	50@6500 rpm
R65	82	61.5	650	8.7:1	48@7250 rpm

BMW equipped the new twins with an attractive but restrictive new exhaust system, with a large welded premuffler interconnecting the left and right exhaust pipes forward of the twin mufflers. This effectively retained the horsepower of the previous engine, but was a claimed 3 decibels quieter. Until October 1985, the R80 and R65 included only a single exhaust gasket. Also different from the previous version was the K-series final drive assembly and its lighter and more substantial casting, with new tapered roller bearings. The R80 final drive ratio was 1:3.20 (10/32). The R80RT and R65 ratio was 1:3.36 (11/37).

From March 1985 there was a new gearbox input shaft, and a new input helical gear driving a new lay shaft with a 17.5-degree gear cut, replacing the previous 15-degree cut. There was also a new gear lever bush and gear cam, with a further modification to the cam from September 1986, and after June 1988 there was a new clutch pushrod and release bearing.

Chassis

In creating the chassis of its revamped boxers, BMW used a combination of R80ST and K-series components. The frame was inherited from the R80ST, with a Monolever swingarm. The steering head angle was 28.85 degrees, providing 4.5 inches (116 mm) of trail. Starting in 1988, this was changed to 27.8 degrees and 4.7 inches (120 mm).

While the frame and swingarm were similar to the R80 G/S and R80ST, the wheels brakes and suspension had more in common with the K series. The fork was a K75-style center-axle 38.5-mm unit, providing considerably less travel than before, 6.87 inches (175 mm). It also incorporated an integral fork brace, a larger diameter hollow axle (1 inch or 25 mm), and provided for forward mounting of the brake calipers. Fork legs for 1985 were plain alloy, but they were painted black from 1986 on. Starting in 1992, BMW began fitting forks by Marzocchi. Only U.S. versions incorporated reflectors in the fork leg.

At the rear was a single gas-charged Boge shock absorber, providing 4.76 inches (121 mm) of travel. At the top, the shock attached to a forged-steel mount on the frame. At the bottom, the shock was attached to the rear drive housing (as on the K series), rather than to the swingarm. The laid-down position resulted in a higher leverage

The 18-inch front wheel and more abbreviated front fender of the post-1984 R80 provided a more up-to-date look. The fork gaiters are nonstandard, but they are a practical addition to the Marzocchi fork fitted to this late example. This is still a very handsome machine, in the style of the pre-1985 standard twins.

Either single or dual front discs were fitted on the post-1984 R80, with the later examples receiving this newer type of Brembo twin-piston caliper. The caliper bodies had different logos, and the right caliper included a metal pipe connector to the left.

ratio than on the R80 G/S and R80ST. As usual on a BMW, the only suspension adjustment was four spring preload settings on the rear shock.

The front and rear cast-alloy MT H 2.50x18-inch wheels were also K series derived, and not unlike the design for the R65LS except that they now accommodated tubeless tires. The Y-fork and H-cross-section were designed to provide spoke elasticity with rim rigidity. The rear wheel incorporated a 200-mm drum brake and the rear hub differed from the R80 G/S and R80ST in that it was fastened to the drive hub by four lug bolts. Starting in September 1989, there was an improved rear drum brake, which increased the brake pad width to 27.5 mm (from 25 mm), and new mounts for the brake shoes.

A very narrow 90/90H18 front tire (usually a Metzeler Perfect ME11) contributed to agile steering without compromising braking performance. However, the stability of the new R80 and R65 at higher speed wasn't as good as the earlier model with the 19-inch front wheel. The rear tire was a reasonably large 120/90H18 (often a Metzeler ME99).

The front brake was upgraded with a larger slotted 285x5-mm disc; a dual-piston, 36-mm Brembo caliper; and a 14-mm master cylinder. American-market twins for 1985 were given twin front discs, but for 1986 and 1987, even the U.S. R80s and R80RTs had only a single front disc as

A welcome addition to the K75-style front fork was an integral fork brace. This is also a Marzocchi (from a 1992 R100RT).

The final R80 retained the smaller-diameter MotoMeter instruments, but with a more convenient location for the ignition switch.

Public demand prompted the return of the classic R100RS in 1986, with regular production commencing the following year. Although there were many improvements over the 1984 edition, the rather garish styling of the 1986–89 version did little to endear it to the R100RS enthusiast. This 1986 version includes the solid front fairing section of the 1984 model. *BMW*

R80RT, R80, and R65 Dimensions, Weights, and Performance (1985–95)

Model	R80RT	R80	R65
Overall width	29.37 inches	29.37 inches	27.1 inches
Saddle height	31.8 inches	32.3 inches	31.8 inches
Overall length	85.6 inches	85.6 inches	85.6 inches
Overall height	58.2 inches	43.6 inches	43.6 inches
Wheelbase	57.0 inches	57.0 inches	57.0 inches
Weight including oil but without fuel	455.4 pounds	419 pounds	402.6 pounds
Weight including oil and fuel	499.4 pounds	462 pounds	451 pounds
Top speed	106 mph	111 mph	108 mph

standard. These single-disc models received R100GS solid discs and a 38-mm Brembo caliper starting in July 1988, and the drilled semifloating type from 1991. All twin-disc versions retained the slotted discs.

While the steel gas tank retained the same classic shape as that of the R100, it now held only 5.8 gallons (22 liters), because some of the electrical components that were previously located inside the headlight shell were moved to the frame backbone. The tank cap was an annoying EPA-mandated spring-loaded type.

There was a narrower seat that also continued the previous theme, but the abbreviated plastic front fender was more angular, and there were new sidecovers that made it easy to visually check the battery acid level. Continuing the classic theme were the smaller diameter MotoMeter instruments, and single, or sometimes twin, round Bosch horns. The ignition switch for the R80 and R65 was moved to the handlebar's protective cover, and new handlebar switches were fitted. Switches for U.S. models didn't include an on/off switch for the headlights. A 21-piece toolkit was standard, as was a 12-volt power socket. The sidestand was improved, and the R80RT fairing now incorporated a clock and voltmeter. As always, accessories were plentiful, extending from panniers and tank bag, to four-way flashers, and a 30-Ah battery.

1987–1995 R100RS, R100RT, and R100

Although demand for the R80, R65, and particularly the R80RT, remained strong in Europe (if not in the United States), there was still a call for the return of the 1,000-cc boxer. Late in 1986 a new R100RS was released for the 1987 model year, initially as a run of 1,000 examples. The response was so positive that the R100RS became a regular model for the 1988 model year and was joined by a new R100RT. Both the R100RS and R100RT made it to the United States for 1988, but they were not greeted with the same enthusiasm as their earlier twin-shock counterparts. Only 599 R100RSs and 980 R100RTs were sold in the United States from 1988 to 1990, although there were further R100RSs for 1992. The R100RT ran through the end of 1995 in the United States, but it was very much a niche market model by that stage. When they came to the United States in 1988, the R100RS and R100RT sold for a heady $7,750, although this was still significantly less than the K100RS and K100RT. For 1991 the regular R100 made a return, but only for the U.S. market. This was essentially an R80 with the R100RS/RT engine and only lasted for one year, as it was replaced by the R100R for 1992. With only 157 produced, it is one of the rarest and most unusual of the modern BMWs.

Engine and Drivetrain

One of the reasons for the lukewarm reception of the resurrected 1,000-cc twins was that the engines were now derived from the R80 and put out 60 horsepower, rather than the 70 horsepower of the old R100RS and RT engines. Long gone were the days of the R90S, with its class-leading Superbike performance. The new 1,000-cc engine was designed to provide more relaxed power over a wider rev range. It was also required to meet new European emissions controls taking effect in 1988, and to run on regular unleaded gas.

Inside the cylinder head were the smaller 42-mm inlet valves of the R80, while the exhausts went up to the 40-mm units of the 1984 980-cc engine. Carburetion was by smaller V64/32/363-4 Bing carburetors, and while the engine power and torque were down, maximum torque of 55 ft-lb was now produced at a low 3,500 rpm.

R100RS and R100RT Engine Specifications (1987–96)

Bore (mm)	Stroke (mm)	Capacity (cc)	Compression Ratio	Horsepower DIN
94	70.6	980	8.45:1	60@6500 rpm

Although on-the-road performance was similar at legal speeds, the new R100RS was noticeably down on top speed. Both the R100RS and R100RT included a standard oil cooler. In respects other than those listed, the new 1,000-cc engine was the same as the R80. There was the same 280-watt alternator, but the electrical system included a larger 30-Ah Mareg battery. Neither the R100RS nor R100RT shared the new electric start of the R100GS (see the next section) so a 3-amp battery charger was included in the specification. Both models also included the 1:3.00 (11/33) final drive ratio of the R80.

Chassis

Carried over from the 1984 R100RS was an identical fairing, but with larger black mirrors and a front section that included the vented grill of the pre-1979 R100RS, along with the oil cooler at the top. The R100RT bodywork was identical to that of the R80RT. The colors were new, with most R100RSs in white for 1988 with rather cheap-looking blue decals. There was also a red R100RS, with similar black decals, and a black lower fairing, and the R100RT was Bermuda blue for the United States in 1988. No hydraulic steering damper was fitted to either model, but the protective pad on the RS was the same as before and looked strange without the damper knob. A round BMW badge sat in its place.

Underneath the RS and RT bodywork was a Monolever chassis similar to that of the newer R80 and R65. For 1988 there was new steering geometry, now with a 27.8-degree steering head angle and 4.7 inches (120 mm) of trail. The front fork was the same K-series type as used on the R80, with 38.5-mm fork tubes. An underdamped single Boge shock absorber provided the rear suspension.

Twin front disc brakes were standard, along with the R80 rear drum, instead of the disc rear brake of the pre-1985 RS. This seemed to be purely a cost-cutting measure, and the disc brake really should have been included for the price. Also the same as the R80 were the wheels, although the R100RS wheels were black with plain-alloy accents. The tire sizes were unchanged from the R80, but included slippery Michelin A/M48s, or superb Continental TKV11/12. Unlike the R80, the R100RS and RT were both fitted with dual Fiamm horns. Two types of saddlebags were optional, the R-type or squarer K-type.

The R100RS front end was very similar to that of the K75S, with similar dual front disc brakes, slotted discs, and center-axle fork.

While providing improved on-the-road performance, the resurrected R100RS lacked many of the quality detail touches that distinguished earlier models. No longer were there specific model emblems on the rear of the seat.

The post-1987 R100RS vented fairing panel in front of the engine was an amalgam of the 1977 and 1979 types. As on the 1979–84 R100RS, an oil cooler was standard, but the new grill-like front panel was kinder to the electrical components, as it allowed more air to circulate in front of the engine.

The cockpit layout was familiar, but the handlebar switches were new, and there was no longer a steering damper.

R100RS and R100RT Dimensions, Weights, and Performance (1986–96)

Model	R100RS	R100RT
Overall width	31.50 inches	37.79 inches
Saddle height	31.8 inches	31.8 inches
Overall length	85.6 inches	85.6 inches
Overall height	54.3 inches	58.2 inches
Wheelbase	57.0 inches	57.0 inches
Weight including oil but without fuel	461 pounds	471 pounds
Weight including oil and fuel	505 pounds	515 pounds
Top speed	116 mph	109 mph

The final R100RS was the Rennsport 30 of 1992. Standard were the K series type of pannier, and chrome-plated engine-protection bars. The twin–spark plug cylinder heads are nonstandard, but provide a beneficial improvement.

Each Rennsport 30 came with this special numbered plaque inside the fairing.

The 1989 version was identical to that of 1988, but there were more subdued colors and decals for 1990 (silver). Only a few were produced during 1990 (337) and 1991 (393), and none came to the United States. As a final fling, 954 were built for 1992, with 151 coming to the United States. These were sold as 1993 models, for $9,340. It now came with a Marzocchi front fork. Colors were metallic black, or metallic pine green, and a series of 30 Rennsport special editions came in traditional blue and silver, with a numbered plaque. The wheels were no longer highlighted black. After the demise of the R100RS in the wake of the oil-head R1100RS, the R100RT continued for a few more years with few changes. U.S. models for 1994 included heated grips, a custom touring seat, and 5.72-gallon (22-liter) rear trunk. For some markets, the R100RT was labeled the R100LT. The R100RT ended with the Classic, offered for 1995 and into 1996.

With its shorter wheelbase, lighter weight, and more rigid frame, the post-1986 R100RS provided more agile and surefooted handling than the earlier version. But the reduction in horsepower did little to endear it to a new breed of enthusiasts. Despite its reintroduction due to popular demand, after 1987, production gradually dwindled. Only 6,081 Monolever R100RSs were produced, with 750 destined for the United States. It was another story with the R100RT, a model that was consistently popular through its last year of production in 1996, with 9,738 produced.

1987–90 R100GS and R80GS

Although the resurrected R100RS failed in its quest to re-create its classic forebear, the rejuvenated R100GS and R80GS not only continued the tradition of the R80 G/S, it expanded and improved the concept of Gelände Strasse. To imply a change in direction to off-road sports, BMW omitted the slash between the G and the S and updated the Monolever chassis to include a double universal joint and Paralever swingarm.

Compared to the previous G/S, the new GS was a significantly larger motorcycle. There were two versions, the R100GS, and R80GS, although only the 1,000-cc model was sold in the United States. The new GS was immediately successful, and during its first two years was the best-selling motorcycle of any brand in Germany.

Engine and Drivetrain

The R100GS engine was basically that of the R100RS and RT. There were 42- and 40-mm valves, with slightly narrower stems (7.95 mm). The R80GS engine was basically that of the R80, but with 40-mm exhaust valves (compared to 38-mm for the R80), with new valve seat angles. Valve guides were also shorter (46.5 mm).

Inside the engine, the oil-pump delivery rate was reduced to 1,399.2 quarts (1,320 liters) per hour (from 1,484 quarts or 1,400 liters) at 6,000 rpm, and the GS retained the smaller sump, but with a larger sump bash plate. Oil capacity was 2.64 quarts (2.25 liters). R100GSs were equipped with a five-row oil cooler, fitted on the black right-side engine protection bar, and the rocker covers were also now black.

R100GSs for Europe were equipped with 40-mm Bing carburetors. American R100 models and all R80GS models had Bing 32-mm carburetors. With the smaller carbs, U.S. R100GSs were less powerful, 58 horsepower instead of 60. Starting in 1989, the carburetors received new slide needles.

The chrome-plated steel exhaust system was different from that of the R80 G/S. Header diameter was 36.05 mm, rear pipe diameter was 38.05 mm, and the presilencer volume was increased to 3.8 liters. The final drive ratio for R100GS was 1:3.09 (11/34) and for the R80GS was 1:3.20 (10/32).

While demand for the R100RS dwindled after a few years, the R100RT continued as a relatively popular model.This is a 1992 example, also looking very similar to its 1979 predecessor. An oil cooler was now standard.

Electrical System and Ignition

There was no change to the electrical system, apart from a rearrangement of the electrical components under the fuel tank, and a smaller starter motor (Valeo D6 RA) with a Wehrle starter relay. This starter included an intermediate 5.5:1 planetary gear (similar to the K series) and its output was 1.1 kW (1.47 horsepower). There was a 4-pound (2 kilogram) weight savings with the new starter setup. Two types of Bosch ignition triggers were fitted to the GS, one with a longer switching duration for models fitted with the now optional kickstart. The battery was a 25-Ah unit instead of the 30-Ah of the R100RS and RT.

The final R100RT was the Classic of 1995 and 1996, complete with luxury saddle, color-matched panniers, and trunk. All final air-cooled boxer twins featured the secondary air injection system.

Chassis

Most of the development was saved for the chassis, and the GS was the first BMW motorcycle to incorporate the now-ubiquitous Paralever

R80GS, R100GS, R100PD, and R100R Carburetors

Model	R80GS (R100GS/PD/R US)	R100GS/PD/R
Left Carburetor	Bing V64 II 64/32/349(351)	Bing V64 II 94/40/123
Right Carburetor	Bing V64 II 64/32/349(352)	Bing V64 II 94/40/124
Main Jet	135 (132)	150
Needle Jet	2.68 (2.66)	2.66
Jet Needle No.	46-251	46-371
Needle Position	3	3
Idle Jet	45	45

R80GS, R100GS, and R100R Engine Specifications (1987–96)

Model	Bore (mm)	Stroke (mm)	Capacity (cc)	Compression Ratio	Horsepower DIN
R100GS/R100R	94	70.6	980	8.5:1	60@6500 rpm
R80GS	84.8	70.6	798	8.2:1	50@6500 rpm

The oil cooler for the R100GS was mounted in the airstream, on the right engine protection bar.

New for the R100GS and R80GS was the Paralever swingarm, a highly successful method of controlling the shaft drive torque reaction on the rear suspension. The Paralever swingarm is now featured on all BMW motorcycles.

swingarm. BMW strengthened the frame, with the oval tubes inside the backbone reinforced, although there was still no double tube, as with the earlier twins, for the new GS. The steering head angle was 28 degrees, with 3.98 inches (101 mm) of trail. There was a stronger rear subframe and built-in luggage rack, along with a redesigned centerstand with more curved-out pedals. A sidestand was integrated with the left engine protection bar of the R100GS, but wasn't standard on the R80GS. But the real chassis news was the second-generation Monolever, the Paralever.

Pressure cast in alloy, the 17.7-inch- (450-mm-) long Paralever swingarm retained the adjustable bevel roller bearing, but included two additional adjustable needle roller bearings between the swingarm and the drive housing. Along with the double universal joints on the driveshaft, the Paralever design minimized the effect of torque reaction on the suspension, providing the effect of a longer swingarm.

The rear gearcase and hub assembly floated on the rear axle, with the movement controlled by an alloy stay arm connecting the bottom of the case to the frame, just below the swingarm pivot. The swingarm, stay arm, gearcase, and frame formed a parallelogram, with pinion torque feeding into the lower strut instead of the swingarm. The slight fore and aft movement of the gearcase was absorbed by the laid-down single shock absorber. Because the parallelogram arrangement increased the radius of the wheel's elevation curve, it provided the same effect as a 55-inch (1,400-mm) swingarm. The weight penalty was only 3.5 pounds (1.6 kilograms).

As on the R80, the shock absorber bolted to the final drive housing. The Paralever allowed the increased travel (7.1 inches or 180 mm) of the Boge gas-pressure shock absorber to be used more effectively. For 1989, BMW softened the action of the softer shock absorber, but the previous unit was still available as an option. For 1990 there was the option of a White Power sports suspension kit, which included replacement fork springs and a new rear shock absorber.

Despite the advantages of the Paralever, it still wasn't perfect, and the two needle roller bearings at the front coupling were especially prone to wear. They could even wear through the coupling yoke before the problem became apparent.

Complementing the Paralever swingarm was a new leading-axle 40-mm Marzocchi fork with low-friction Teflon-coated sleeves, thicker aluminum triple clamps, fork brace, and a hollow 25-mm axle. The fork springs were 445 mm and the longer tubes contained more fluid (470 cc). Fork gaiters were standard, and the nonadjustable dampers featured larger orifices. Spring travel was increased to 225 mm (8.86 inches). The fork legs were also painted yellow on the Avus black GS, but black for Alpine white and Marrakesh red versions, and they incorporated side reflectors. The black GS also featured a yellow spring for the shock absorber.

The GS wheels were an innovative wire-spoke type allowing tubeless tires for the first time. These cross-spoked wheels featured straight-pull spokes laced from the extreme edges of the rim, with the adjusting nipples in the hub. The crosswise arrangement of the spokes was claimed to increase torsional rigidity, and they permitted replacing or adjusting spokes without removing the wheel. As on the R80, the rear wheel was retained by four lug nuts. The aluminum rims were 1.85x21-inch MTH2 on the front, and a 2.50x17-inch MTH2 on the rear. Newer generation tubeless Metzeler Sahara tires were 90/90S21 and 130/80S17. The front brake on the GS was a single undrilled 285x6-mm disc, with a Brembo twin 38-mm piston caliper and a 13-mm master cylinder. The rear brake was a 200-mm drum, which was now cable, rather than rod, actuated.

All the bodywork was new for the GS. The 5.8-gallon (26-liter) fuel tank, was 1 inch shorter than that of the R80 G/S, and included a larger (81-mm) round BMW emblem and twin petcocks. Except on some early examples, the gas cap was now vented, without a vent tube. As the GS was promoted as an effective tarmac machine as well as an off-road explorer, from 1989 BMW provided both upper and lower mounting points for the front fender.

The sparse instrument layout, rubber-mounted to the top triple clamp, was similar to that of the previous G/S. The single speedometer was flanked on the right by a series of warning lights. The R100GS included a taller nacelle above the 140-mm headlight, while the R80GS headlight nacelle was lower. The black-chrome handlebar was 32.37 inches (830 mm). Handlebar switches were of the other post-1985 R series. The footpegs and levers followed the style of the R80 G/S pegs and levers, but the rear brake lever was redesigned for 1990. For those riders who felt the R100GS was too low, there was an even higher 34.6-inch (880-mm) seat available.

Cross-spoke wheels not only provided increased rigidity, they also allowed the fitting of tubeless tires. Spoke adjustment was at the hub. As with the R80, the rear hub was retained by four lug nuts.

Providing increased travel, the 40-mm Marzocchi front fork of the R100GS was an improvement over that of the R80 G/S but was still nonadjustable. The single front disc was solid through 1990.

1990 R100GS Paris-Dakar

During 1989, a Paris-Dakar kit was produced for the R80GS and R100GS, and for 1990 BMW offered the R100GS Paris-Dakar as a regular-production model, alongside the R80GS and R100GS. At $7,860 it was the most expensive dirt bike available, and it was also the largest. However, despite its intimidating size, the Paris-Dakar was an extremely successful niche model, particularly in Europe, because there was nothing else like it available, and it suited largerframed riders.

Continuing the theme of the earlier R80 G/S Paris-Dakar, the R100GS Paris-Dakar was essentially an R100GS with cosmetic attire. This centered on a huge fiberglass 9.3-gallon (35-liter) fuel tank that featured the racing bike's graphics, and incorporated a lockable 5.3-quart (5-liter) storage cavity. As the huge gas tank lacked the mandatory gas-vapor emissions canister required for California, the Paris-Dakar wasn't available in that state, although the Paris-Dakar kit could be bought separately.

Along with this fuel tank, the Paris-Dakar was equipped with a reinforced fiberglass fairing attached to both the handlebar and frame. The fairing side sections connected to the fuel tank, and there was a tinted windshield. The tubular fairing support was external, and incorporated a rectangular K75S headlight with grill-like rock guard for protection. In addition to the standard GS instrument layout, the Paris-Dakar included a small tachometer and matching quartz clock.

The Paris-Dakar R100GS appeared for 1990, looking unlike any other motorcycle. Prominent features were an external tubular-steel fairing support that incorporated a headlight protector, and a large alloy sump protection plate. The Paris-Dakar may have been big, but it was a competent adventure tourer that made getting away from it all very easy. The rectangular panniers were an option.

New for the Paris-Dakar was an instrument panel that included a small tachometer and clock. The rider sat up high, but the wide handlebar provided a feeling of security in rough going.

Although the Paris-Dakar fiberglass gas tank held 9.3 gallons (35.24 liters), there was room for this lockable storage compartment in the top. Large enough for maps and documents, it contributed to the practicality of the Paris-Dakar as an adventure tourer.

Other specific Paris-Dakar components were a larger aluminum sump protector, also covering the frame and exhaust system, and mounted to the sump with rubber silence blocks. A plastic protective cover fitted around the engine protection bars, and wider aluminum reinforced sections bolted to the stock R100GS front fender. A solo seat with longer luggage rack was standard, although the R100GS dual seat and rack were also available. Unlike the seat of the earlier Paris-Dakar, the solo seat of the new Paris-Dakar was more easily removed. A unique touch was the availability of the Paris-Dakar gas tank in plain primer paint, allowing the owner to add customized paintwork. U.S. models also came standard with black tubular steel saddlebag mounts, although the rectangular bags were optional.

1991–96 R100GS, R80GS, and R100GS Paris-Dakar

After 10 years of production and sales of more than 50,000, the GS lineup was revamped for 1991 with a subtle emphasis more toward road use. While the engine was unchanged but for a larger (2.64-quart or 2.5-liter) sump and stainless-steel muffler, there were a number of chassis updates. Standard on all versions were the frame-mounted cockpit fairing and external tubular frame of the 1990 R100GS Paris-Dakar. This fairing included a rectangular headlight and an adjustable windshield that could tilt back and forth 3 inches (75 mm). There was a new instrument layout, now with a large speedometer and tachometer, and the handlebar switches were from the K series with separate switches on either side for the turn-signals. The turn-signals weren't self-canceling, because the GS speedometer wasn't electronic.

Adjusters for the steering head bearings used the finer thread of the K75. The Bilstein rear shock absorber was now adjustable for 10 positions of rebound damping. The front brake was also upgraded to include a thinner (285x5-mm) semifloating front rotor, new brake pads, and a 13-mm master cylinder. There was a new, smaller, 25.44-quart (24-liter) fuel tank for the GS, with a lockable, flush-mounted filler cap. To further emphasize street use, the front fender

Subtle changes to the R100GS and Paris-Dakar for 1991 moved the focus toward the street and away from dirt. The 1991 Paris-Dakar looked very similar to the 1990 version, but there was now a low front fender. The plastic hand protectors were retained.

was mounted low over the tire. The seat was also tougher, with different foam.

As release of the new R1100GS grew imminent, BMW made no further changes to the R100GS and R80GS, apart from some very garish graphics and colors, until production ended in 1996.

Nevertheless, BMW offered a "farewell model" of the R100GS, the R100GS PD Classic for 1994 and 1995, in Avus Black with a black dual seat. The fairing support and engine protection bars were chrome-plated, and the handlebar levers were coated in silver epoxy. There was a wider, high-mounted front mudguard, the older R68-style round rocker covers, and heated handlebar grips, and all models came with the SAS secondary air induction system.

The R80GS continued for 1996 as the R80GS Basic, primarily for the German market. Essentially an earlier R80GS with a small fuel tank and headlight cowl, the colors were white, with a blue frame, Paralever swingarm, and the round rocker covers. An R80GS Basic was also the final air-cooled boxer produced, the last leaving the Spandau production line on December 19, 1996.

Providing exemplary road performance and acceptable off-road agility, the GS had established itself as the most popular post-1984 air-cooled boxer twin, and the archetypal adventure tourer; 45,364 were produced. It paved the way for the equally successful R1100GS and R1150GS. Even in the wake of this new, larger, and heavier, "oil-head" GS, the older R100GS remained a wonderful and competent all-purpose motorcycle.

The standard R100GS was now in garish colors, and received many Paris-Dakar components, including the fairing. The screen was adjustable, and the fuel tank smaller than before, with a flush-mounted filler cap. There was a large tachometer alongside the speedometer, and the handlebar switches were from the K series. Whether this was an improvement was debatable, but the R100GS was still a very popular motorcycle. *BMW*

R100GS, R100GS PD, and R80GS Dimensions, Weights, and Performance (1987–96)

Model	R100GS	R100GS PD	R80GS
Overall width	32.7 inches	32.7 inches	32.7 inches
Saddle height	33.5 inches	33.5 inches	33.5 inches
Overall length	90.2 inches	90.2 inches	90.2 inches
Overall height	45.9 inches	45.9 inches	45.9 inches
Wheelbase	59.6 inches	59.6 inches	59.6 inches
Weight including oil but without fuel	433 pounds (455 pounds 1991)	433 pounds (455 pounds 1991)	411 pounds (422 pounds 1991)
Weight including oil and fuel	484 pounds (519 pounds 1991)	484 pounds (519 pounds 1991)	462 pounds (473 pounds 1991)
Top speed	112 mph	112 mph	104 mph

New for 1991 was a semifloating drilled front disc brake, although the dual-piston Brembo caliper was retained.

From 1991 the Paris-Dakar instrument panel was the same as the R100GS, but with a white plastic surround.

1992–96 R100R, R80R, and Mystic

While the world was still waiting for the new generation "oil-head" R259 during 1992, with its release more than a year away, the R100R Roadster was created out of the R100GS for 1992. Designed as a classic-look "grassroots" machine to maintain interest in the boxer lineage, the R100R proved extremely successful. In its first year of manufacture it was the most popular BMW motorcycle, with 8,041 sales accounting for nearly 23 percent of BMW's worldwide production. The R100R shamed the much-vaunted four-valve K series, but while there was no denying the functional superiority of the R100R chassis over that of earlier boxer street bikes, the styling and execution was questionable. A proliferation of gaudy and cheap components detracted from what could have been one of the classic BMW motorcycles, as did the parts-bin nature of its execution.

Engine and Drivetrain

In the style of the R80ST, the R100R used the dual-purpose R100GS as a basis. But for a different exhaust system and a return to the older-style (R68 through to /6) rocker covers, the R100R engine was identical to that of the R100GS. This included the larger sump of the 1991 GS and the layshaft starter. European versions featured 40-mm Bing carburetors, while the U.S. models retained 32-mm carburetors. The chrome-plated exhaust header pipes were 38 mm, and fed into the large premuffler and low-mounted stainless steel K100 muffler. Instead of mounting the seven-row oil cooler on the engine protection bar as on the GS, this was now positioned in front of the engine. The classic look even extended to the older-style spark plug caps, but the engine was still surprisingly similar to the 1981 version.

Chassis

Also from the R100GS was the frame (now painted silver) and Paralever swingarm. This was the first street boxer twin to include the Paralever, and it contributed to outstanding street manners. While the steering geometry was unchanged, different wheels and suspension resulted in a shorter wheelbase. In a major departure for BMW, Japanese Showa suspension was used front and rear, the shorter nonadjustable 41-mm front fork providing 5.3 inches (135 mm) of travel. The fluid capacity of 420 cc was less than that of the GS' Marzocchi fork. The single Showa shock absorber provided 5.5 inches (140 mm) of travel, seven steps of adjustment for spring preload, and a screw to adjust rebound damping. As with most mass-produced Showa shock absorbers, these worked adequately when new, but lost their damping over time.

Further emphasizing the classic "retro" image were cross-spoked wheels, with Akront aluminum rims. The rim sizes were 2.50x18-inch MTH2 on the front, and 2.50x17-inch MTH2 on the rear, allowing a 110/80V18 front tire (Metzeler ME33 Laser) and 140/80V17 rear tire (Metzeler ME55A Metronic). The front brake was a single perforated floating 285x5-mm disc, with a four-piston Brembo caliper from the K series. The cable-operated rear drum was the same as that of the GS. Also from the GS was the 5.7-gallon (24-liter) fuel tank, which looked too large and tall. The handlebar cover, sidecovers, passenger grab handle, and rear fender were unique to the R100R.

The round 180-mm headlight came from the K75, but with a chrome shell. Situated in a cheap plastic housing were the instruments from the R100GS, while the 28.08-inch (720-mm) chrome-plated handlebar was similar to that of the R80ST,

Created out of the R100GS as a retro machine, the R100R was BMW's most popular motorcycle during 1992. There was only a single front disc brake on this early example, and the frame was painted silver. The Brembo four-piston caliper was from the K1100RS.

With its older style round rocker covers and metal-shrouded spark plug caps, the R100R engine looked similar to a pre-1977 boxer twin. Even the fuel petcocks are the older style. This is a later Mystic, but the engine was identical to that of the R100R.

with K series handlebar switches and end weights to minimize vibration. The foot controls were also similar to those of the GS, with the same reversed gear shift linkage. The colors for 1992 were classic black, or amethyst, both with a two-tone seat and silver rear rack. If those looks were too subdued, there was also an optional chrome kit. This comprised a chrome-plated fork stabilizer, valve covers, carburetor tops, instrument panel, turn-signal housings, fuel tank cap, mirrors, and exhaust nuts.

With the formula of the moderately powered, light, and simple twin firmly established, BMW made only cosmetic changes to the R100R for 1993. It was also joined by a similar R80R, in 34- and 50-horsepower versions without an oil cooler. The R80R wasn't sold in the United States and only lasted until 1994. Setting the 1993 R100R (and R80R) apart were large, and particularly inconspicuous, BOXER emblems on the sides of the gas tank of the new turquoise green metallic examples. This retained the silver frame and rear rack, while the R100R in black now had a black frame and rack.

The R100R engine may have continued an earlier tradition, but the Paralever swingarm from the R100GS was very up to date, and provided the R100R with excellent handling. The rear drum brake was cable-operated.

For 1994 the R100R received a black-painted frame, black rear rack, and dual-disc front brakes. The two-tone seat was retained, and U.S. examples like this featured fork-leg reflectors. The styling was fussy and unsuccessful, and the R100R was a missed opportunity to create a real retro classic. All versions now included the SAS exhaust port air injection. *Cycle World*

Extending the classic image was the Mystic, with more chrome and a restyled seat and tailpiece. This was certainly a more successful styling exercise than the regular R100R, but the gas tank was still too tall. Despite offering functional superiority over earlier examples, by 1995 time had run out for the air-cooled boxer.

For 1994 the R100R received dual-disc front brakes, all versions now had the SAS emissions system standard, and there was a special Mystic version. The Mystic was designed to appeal to the connoisseur of classic motorcycles, and on it many of the dubious features of the R100R were replaced. Along with the special red metallic paint, was a chrome-plated headlight support, a metal chrome-plated instrument surround with new warning light console, chrome-plated turn signal supports, a lower handlebar, restyled seat and tailpiece, black-painted frame, new sidecovers, and a shorter license plate support. The muffler was also turned 3 centimeters to the inside along the longitudinal axis. The R80R was discontinued at the end of model year 1994.

The R100R and Mystic continued for 1995 and into 1996, the R100R now titled the R100R Classic. Only in black, this featured more cosmetic variation, including a black seat, headlight support, instrument console, and grab handle. The handlebar levers were silver epoxy.

There was no denying that the retrospective roadster formula was outstandingly successful, as naked motorcycles were becoming more popular. The excellent handling provided by the light weight and Paralever swingarm, combined with the reliability and moderate power of the well-proven A10 boxer engine was a powerful attraction. They may have been parts-bin specials, without the grace of the earlier R100s (or even the later R80), but the naked R100R and R80R models were among the most popular BMW motorcycles of the 1990s. Over the six years they were in production, 24,128 R100Rs and R80Rs were produced.

R100R Dimensions, Weights, and Performance (1992–96)

	R100R
Overall width	28.3 inches
Saddle height	31.5 inches
Overall length	87 inches
Overall height	46.8 inches
Wheelbase	58.8 inches
Weight including oil but without fuel	433 pounds
Weight including oil and fuel	480 pounds
Top speed	112 mph

Chapter 11

Living with an Air-Cooled Boxer Twin

There are few vintage motorcycles that are as useable as an air-cooled BMW boxer twin. Long model runs, and the continued availability of parts, makes a boxer an eminently practical proposition, even in the wake of the newer "oil-head" twins. With the factory under the Mobile Tradition banner, still providing spare parts for older models—even restoration to original specification—is feasible.

Reliability is never really an issue with a BMW because the air-cooled boxer engine is one of the most reliable of all motorcycle designs. These engines just refuse to die. They may not be perfect, but there are few other classic motorcycles that offer comparable performance and all-around capability, and can be relied upon to run for hundreds of thousands of miles. The post-1969 M04*, M65*, and A10 engines were not only the longest-lived of all BMW motorcycle units, but amassed a huge following of loyal supporters. If an air-cooled boxer gives any problems, it will more likely be the transmission or other drivetrain components. As already described, the boxer was continually developed over its 27-year lifespan, although this development slowed considerably after 1984. These myriad incremental improvements saw the air-cooled boxer evolve into an extremely reliable motorcycle. And because the basic engine architecture was

Even classic boxer models, such as this 1976 R90S owned by the author, are extremely useable and reliable motorcycles. In this case the choice of machine was governed by nostalgia and aesthetics. It is easy to see why the R90S has earned a classic status and garnered a significant following.

One of the most famous, and highly modified, air-cooled boxers was Steve McLaughlin's 1976 Daytona Superbike race winner. The chassis featured a cantilever monoshock swingarm, and engine developments extended to shorter cylinders for increased ground clearance. With this motorcycle, the image of BMW motorcycles as staid and boring touring machines was shattered forever. *Bruce Armstrong*

It is possible to successfully modify a boxer while retaining the original appearance. This 1992 Rennsport 30 R100RS has twin-plug cylinder heads and a Koni rear shock absorber, yet these modifications are unobtrusive.

unchanged, many of the later developments can be retrofitted.

It can also be assumed that a high proportion of the more than 430,000 air-cooled boxer twins produced are still in active service. Unlike some other motorcycles of the era, no air-cooled BMW is too rare to ride. Even the more collectable models, such as the R75/5, R90S, early R100RS, and R80 G/S, were produced in significant numbers. And one thing that distinguishes all the post-1969 twins is that they still don't feel like ancient motorcycles. They were designed for touring, with provision for excellent standard or aftermarket luggage, so any boxer twin can comfortably undertake an interstate or intercontinental journey. A few judicious modifications can also enhance the experience. These don't necessarily need to alter the motorcycle visually, but can be hidden and practical, maintaining the classic profile without too much impediment.

The choice of model may be a result of practical, financial, aesthetic, or even nostalgic considerations. In my own case, the purchase of a Daytona Orange R90S was prompted by my recollection of these machines back in 1976. Not only was the R90S the first BMW with Superbike performance, the victory in the Daytona Superbike race provided BMW with a new image. The R90S was as fast as a Kawasaki 900-cc Z1, but vastly more comfortable and better handling. It may not have possessed the sharp handling or brakes of an Italian sportsbike, but the R90S was in another league when it came to reliability.

I also admit to being a traditionalist, preferring spoked wheels, round engine covers, and metal components to plastic. For me, the R90S represents the finest attributes of the air-cooled boxer and is the classic, modern BMW. However, all larger capacity versions can provide a similar experience, although there was also a noticeable deterioration in quality after the demise of the /6 series. The paintwork was less consistent, as was the overall finish, while the rear disc brake and "snowflake" cast wheels seemingly provided no advantage over the early drum and wire-spoked wheels. Although the /5 and /6 distinguish the era before real cost-cutting was evident, the more modern examples are definitely easier to live with, and they handle better. There were undoubted improvements from 1981, and the 1981–84 examples are probably the epitome of the series despite the foibles of the awkward switchgear, cast wheels, and lower engine performance of U.S. examples.

With a proliferation of models and continual evolution, it isn't possible to detail every fault and solve every problem of the boxer twin, but here is a brief summary of some of the pitfalls and their solutions. It must also be remembered that compared with just about every other motorcycle, the boxer twin is a paragon of reliability, with most problems only evident after extremely high mileage, tortuous and arduous use, or poor maintenance. And this isn't a substitute for a workshop manual.

Engine

With the most powerful stock boxer producing a conservative 70 horsepower, this is well within the engine's design parameters. Although more power is always desirable, the 67- and 70-horsepower engines of the R90S and R100RS feel about right for the chassis and provide acceptable performance. The 750-, 800-, 900-, and 1,000-cc models are all very similar, so it is extremely easy to convert a pre-1981 model to a larger capacity, as the barrels can be rebored.

There were actually very few motorcycles of the early to mid-1970s that performed as strongly as the R90S or early R100RS and R100S. They were certainly the kings of the twins, and it was only when the Japanese manufacturers upped the performance ante in 1978 with the Kawasaki Z1-R, Honda CBX six-cylinder, Yamaha XS1100, and Suzuki GS1000, that the BMW was really overtaken. Unfortunately, in the United States if not in Europe, the performance disparity increased even further after 1979 when the BMW twins were detuned to cope with low-octane fuel. Probably one of the reasons the earlier models have garnered such a following is because their performance was superior. To return horsepower to the level of those earlier days will require high-compression pistons, and possibly a twin–spark plug conversion. As the 1,000-cc engine in particular has an extremely large bore, pre-ignition can be a problem. A second spark plug opposite the original, firing simultaneously, can alleviate this. A byproduct of twin plugs is decreased fuel consumption due to increased combustion efficiency, and a smother idle. Twin plugging is a relatively straightforward procedure, although pre-1981 models will probably require an electronic ignition unit with special twin output coils.

It is unlikely your engine will suffer from a serious malady, although crankshaft and big-end failure isn't unheard of. Also, some pre-1976 engines were known to break flywheel bolts, and rear main seals failed on early models. One of the problems with running a pre-1985 BMW is recession of the valve seats, caused by prolonged high-speed use on lead-free fuel. The hardened valve seats fitted after 1981 were not as effective as claimed, and it is recommended that you replace the valve seats with the type fitted after 1985. As the stock valves are two-piece, with the stems inertia-welded to the heads, they also have a limited life, although this is around 60,000 miles. Another popular recommendation for models after 1976 is to fit the post-1985 rocker kit, which is quieter and requires less maintenance. Cylinder heads of the /5 and early /6 can also be modified to accept this rocker upgrade, but the conversion requires new rocker arms, axles, needle bearings, and pillars.

Many were skeptical when the dual-row timing chain was replaced by a single-row chain in 1979, and their fears were justified. The single-row chain can become very noisy in less than 30,000 miles, as the tensioner blade doesn't provide any tensioning after initial wear. On some post-1984 boxers, the tensioner failed in less than 10,000 miles. Later, an improved plastic tensioner was installed, and this can be retrofitted. Cylinder base oil leaks generally come from the pushrod grommets.

The 1976 Butler and Smith Daytona Superbikes were incredibly modified so as to produce around 100 horsepower. There were 95-mm pistons, twin-plug cylinder heads, and Dell'Orto carburetors bored to 40 mm. In order to save weight, the complete electric start and air box assembly on top of the crankcases were removed. Frame rigidity was also improved with a brace running from the front downtube to the swingarm pivot. *Bruce Armstrong*

Carburetors

Undoubtedly some of the performance superiority of the R90S over other versions is due to its Dell'Orto carburetors. With their accelerator pumps, the Dell'Ortos provide more immediate throttle response but require regular synchronization. The throttle slides are also prone to wear after prolonged use, as the accelerator pump lever rocks the slide in the carburetor body. Most problems with the Bing carburetors are caused by

Aftermarket fork braces can improve the front-end rigidity of earlier models like this R90S, without detracting too much from aesthetics.

damaged or torn diaphragms, and worn needle jets. The needle jets wear as the needles vibrate, with the later brass needles more susceptible, and will probably require replacement every 35,000 miles. Leaking Bing carburetors are a perennial problem, caused by the float-needle rubber tips hardening over time. Another cause of poor performance is incorrect float height. Leaking float chamber gaskets will inhibit cold starting. Blocked choke jets caused by corrosion in the float chamber will also result in engine cutout after starting.

Exhaust Systems

While the stock exhaust system is attractive and efficient, one of its drawbacks is rusting. Repeated short trips can result in condensation forming on the cold spots, and as the internal muffler assembly is attached to the thinly chromed external tubing, it rusts prematurely. Aftermarket mufflers look similar to the factory items, although they may emit a throatier sound, and a stainless-steel exhaust system is considerably more durable.

Clutch, Gearbox, and Final Drive

One of the main weaknesses of the air-cooled boxer is the gearbox and rear drive, and these components were also continually developed over the lifespan of the motorcycle. Collapsed gearbox bearings, input shaft and fifth-gear failure, and fork problems are particularly evident on pre-1978 examples. Loss of fifth gear is usually the result of the front output shaft bearing disintegrating. Jumping out of gear can result if the small cam plate roller or spring breaks. Repairing this will require a complete gearbox overhaul. On pre-1981 models, the clutch free play must be kept in adjustment, or the clutch release bearing will fail prematurely. Considerable effort was spent over the years to improve gear selection, and some improvements, such as the improved gear cam from 1985, can be retrofitted. Emulsified oil in the gearbox is usually a result of water entering through the outside of the speedometer cable.

On twin-shock models, wear on the output splines that drive the rear wheel is a serious (and expensive) problem. Every time the rear wheel is removed, the splines should be cleaned and lubricated with spline lubricant. This was improved for the Monolever R80 G/S and R80ST, and subsequent Monolever models. The clutch splines are also not immune to failure, and these can sometimes tear out of the clutch center if they are not sufficiently lubricated.

The ultimate front end for a pre-1981 boxer as fitted to the Butler and Smith racers later in the 1976 season. The fork brace is massive, and twin-piston Lockheed brake calipers replace the ATE calipers that were used at Daytona. These racers also had 18-inch front wheels as racing tires only came in that size at the time. *Bruce Armstrong*

Electrical System and Ignition

Although the electrical system is similar for all models, and fairly straightforward, there can be a few troubles. Early model diode boards were mounted on flexible mounts that over time can allow the battery cable to short circuit against the inside of the front engine cover. Diode board failure was more prevalent on the 1979–84 RSs with the closed front grill. Battery life is another concern, and it is a good idea to keep the battery on a constant trickle charge when the bike isn't in use. This can be done via the power socket on later models. The flexible battery mounts under the carrier will also deteriorate over time.

It is also important that the battery charge warning-light circuit isn't broken, as if this is broken the alternator will not excite until 5,000 rpm. Over time the alternator brushes leave a residue that can conduct current across the holder and away from the rotor. The brushes should be cleaned periodically, and will require replacing at around 40,000 miles. Even though it may appear weak by modern standards, compared to other motorcycles of the era the alternator was acceptable, and strong enough to power some additional accessories. Voltage regulators can also be problematic, and the contacts on the earlier electromechanical type may require cleaning. Later electronic regulators will require replacement if the alternator voltage increases rapidly while the engine is running.

A problem with earlier models was points failure, often caused by water impregnation or poor maintenance. Pre-1979 models were also prone to wear on the automatic advance unit's retard cam that actuated the points, resulting in inaccurate timing. Ignition-advance units also become problematic with age, as the springs struggle to move seized bob weights. One of the superior features of the post-1981 examples was the Bosch electronic ignition, and failure of this is rare. In isolated cases it may fail through overheating, after the heat transfer paste dries out. Several aftermarket electronic ignition systems are available for points models. Some, like the Newtronic, retain the mechanical advance, while others such as Boyer-Bransden employ a micro digital system. Although the standard high-tension leads are of excellent quality, their exposure to extremes of heat and the elements can result in shorting between the high-tension terminal and steel shroud on the plug caps over time.

Frame

As von der Marwitz decided to incorporate "designed flex" in the /5 frame, the boxer twin always suffered from marginal frame rigidity. This was compounded by the bolted-on rear subframe, lightweight upper triple clamp, and soft, long-travel suspension. In 1969 tires were narrow, hard, and long-wearing, and the /5's focus was on comfortable touring, rather than sporting prowess. As the power increased and tires improved, the demands changed toward sport touring, yet chassis development was still minimal. Frame bracing in 1977 provided some improvement, as did the Monolever swingarm in 1981. Undoubtedly the post-1984 Monolever and Paralever twins provide the sharpest handling, as not only was the swingarm stiffer, the shock absorber fed directly into the main frame, rather than into the bolted-on rear subframe. With the introduction of Marzocchi and Showa forks in 1992, the handling was finally up to date, but it had taken more than 20 years.

Nevertheless, earlier boxers can be made to handle acceptably, without resorting to expensive modifications, such as the cantilever Monoshock swingarm that distinguished the Butler and Smith R90Ss at Daytona in 1976. A common modification on pre-1977 models is to include the additional brace between the two front downtubes, and the stronger swingarm. A braced swingarm was a popular performance modification for boxer twins during the 1980s, and all twin-shock models would benefit from a strengthened rear subframe.

One of the most effective methods of improving handling is correctly tensioning steering head and swingarm bearings. All BMWs are susceptible to weaving caused by overtightness of the steering head bearings, and while the swingarm bearings are a quality tapered roller type, they also require the correct preload to avoid a hinge-in-the-frame feeling. Another problem with all BMWs is the centerstand. It is made of tubular steel and can rust, and pre-1981 stands can loosen on their pivot bolts, wearing and twisting the threads in the frame lugs. The spring-loaded self-retracting sidestands have always been problematic, and difficult to use while seated on the bike. Aftermarket stands that don't automatically fly up are an improvement.

Another traditional weakness of the standard BMW front end is the pressed-steel upper triple clamp. The Butler and Smith R90S racing Superbikes featured a substantial machined aluminum top triple clamp. *Bruce Armstrong*

An optional clock and voltmeter are popular additions to the basic unfaired models.

One advantage BMW motorcycles enjoy over other makes is the continued availability of factory literature, such as owners' and workshop manuals. This contributes to the practicality of owning and using an older motorcycle.

Suspension and Wheels

While the soft, long-travel stock fork and shock absorbers of pre-1985 boxer twins contributed to a wonderful touring ride, this suspension was found wanting as the focus of the twin became more sporting. Not only did the long fork travel contribute to excessive dive under braking, the suspension was too soft, leading to wallowing. Marginal damping, particularly at the rear, compounded all this, doing little to encourage spirited riding.

The first step at improving fork performance was to install aftermarket fork springs, with a progressive spring favored, as it prevented bottoming and alleviated the dive under braking. Additional

When fitted with a windshield, driving lights, dual front disc brakes, and panniers, the R80/7 could rival an R100RT in touring competence.

springs inserted at the bottom of each fork leg could further reduce dive, as could heavier weight fork oil. The stock 5-weight oil was generally considered too light, while 10-weight inhibited action. A good compromise was a mixture to create a 7.5-weight. Fork seal failure on pre-1985 boxers with exposed fork tubes is also a problem, particularly on touring bikes where the fork legs pick up bugs and dirt. This can be solved through fitting the gaiters of the /5 and /6.

Not only did the front fork provide an excessively soft action, the thin 36-mm tubes and stamped-steel upper triple clamp were hardly paragons of strength. Little can be done inexpensively to strengthen the fork tubes, but an aftermarket stainless-steel or aluminum upper triple clamp can definitely improve the rigidity of the front end. Another common modification is installing a steel aftermarket fork brace just above the fender, but this isn't as effective as a stronger top triple clamp.

The standard Boge shock absorbers also suffered from weak springs and limp damping, but this is more easily rectified. Even with the demise of the popular Koni 7610P units, a wide range of aftermarket shock absorbers is available for the twin-shock models. It is even possible to obtain look-alike Boge shock absorbers that provide superior performance. Wheel bearings can also present a problem if not properly adjusted.

Brakes

One of the inferior aspects of the earlier twins was the braking system, particularly on pre-1981 bikes. BMW persevered with a front drum brake on the /5 long after other manufacturers had discarded it, and when it installed a front-disc setup, it was marginal. With a small-diameter stainless steel disc, it suffered in comparison to other European motorcycles. The swinging ATE caliper, and the remote location of the front master cylinder underneath the fuel tank compounded this. The brake caliper pivot spindles were prone to seizing due to corrosion, and the master cylinder Bowden operating cable needed regular adjustment to compensate for stretch. While the dual-disc setup of the R90S was better, especially the later version with perforated discs and larger caliper pistons, the braking performance was still inferior to the better Italian systems.

There is no doubt that BMW took a big step forward with brakes when it fitted Brembo calipers to the front discs from 1981. Another step forward was the relocation of the front master cylinder to the handlebar, but the front disc diameter remained small. Alternative brake pads can optimize the performance of all braking setups, and a popular modification is braided-steel brake lines to provide a more direct brake action. One advantage of the post-1984 twins was a superior braking system, the final R100R receiving the best of all.

Miscellaneous Accessories

BMW pioneered the factory accessory catalog, and a vast array of optional equipment was available, even from the first /5 of 1969. Most of these accessories were of excellent quality, in particular the optional hard luggage. First supplied by Krauser with Denfeld tubular steel brackets, BMW's luggage set the standard for motorcycle bags during the 1970s. Although their shape compromised capacity, with lids that would occasionally spring open while on the move. And they came with a universal Krauser lock. Still, this was superior to other hard luggage available. After January 1983, BMW began using larger Krauser bags with improved locks and individual keys, but the rectangular BMW bags of the same era were less satisfactory. These would sometimes break away from their brackets, resulting in considerable damage if this happened at high speed. Most of the pannier problems were solved with the K-series bag; it was large and secure, and it provided good (if fiddly) locks. Aftermarket luggage by other manufacturers has also been widely available for many years, some of it superior to the factory equipment.

In addition to the factory bags there was always a range of official optional equipment available, and much of this has already been described. Most popular were extra lights and gauges. Aftermarket accessories filled a void the factory didn't provide, including more comfortable seats and a taller windshield for the R100RS. One thing was certain: an air-cooled BMW boxer twin could be fitted out to suit any purpose. These are motorcycles to be ridden and enjoyed, without intimidating the owner through complexity and advanced technology.

Index